MCQs for the New MRCPsych Part II

Other Examination Preparation Books Published by Petroc Press:

Obtainable from all good booksellers or, in case of difficulty, from
Plymbridge Distributors Limited, Plymbridge House, Estover Road,
PLYMOUTH, Devon PL6 7PZ. Tel. 01752–202300; FAX 01752–203333

MCQs for the New MRCPsych Part II

Bangaru Raju, MD, MRCPsych, DPM
Consultant Psychiatrist
St. Mary's Hospital, Castlebar, Co. Mayo, Ireland

Michael Reilly, MRCPsych, DipMang
Clinical Research Fellow
St. Brigid's Hospital, Ballinasloe, Co. Galway, Ireland

David Browne, MB, BCh, DCP
Psychiatric Registrar
St. Mary's Hospital, Castlebar, Co. Mayo, Ireland

Shauna Glynn, MB, BCh, DCP
Psychiatric Registrar
Psychiatric Unit, University College Hospital, Galway, Ireland

PETROC PRESS

Petroc Press, an imprint of LibraPharm Limited

Distributors

Plymbridge Distributors Limited, Plymbridge House, Estover Road, Plymouth
PL6 7PZ, UK

First edition 2002
Reprinted 2002

Published in the United Kingdom by
LibraPharm Limited
Gemini House
162 Craven Road
Newbury
Berkshire
RG14 5NR

A catalogue record for this book is available from the British Library

ISBN 1 900603 63 2

Printed and bound in the United Kingdom by AlphaGraphics, Preston Farm,
Stockton-on-Tees TS18 3TR

Dedication

For our patients

Contents

Introduction

The Chinese curse condemning one to live in interesting times has become almost a cliché, but its reference to the angst that uncertainty can engender remains true. The changes that the Royal College of Psychiatrists has introduced into the MRCPsych examination have been extensive. We have become used to the idea that the multiple-choice question (MCQ) papers are no longer negatively marked, thus a whole generation of advice regarding the proportion of questions one should attempt or guess has been rendered obsolete. Even the term 'MCQ' has almost become a misnomer: the new papers are properly termed the *individual statement papers*. The practical upshot of the latter change has been to increase potentially the number of topics that can be examined from around 50 to 200. This can be challenging: necessitating a greater mental agility to cover a greater range of topics in a limited space of time. It can, however, have advantages: if one knows nothing about a given question, it represents only 0.5% of the total mark, and one has an evens chance of getting it right anyway by guessing.

At the time of writing, the individual statement papers have been implemented. Candidates noted from the first sittings that the College had used the practical method of simply breaking down the old stem-and-item questions from the bank into 2–3 similar items in many cases. This overlap of questions is likely to continue until such time that newly written individual statements have been built up in the question bank. This shortage of material in the early days of a changed examination format is mirrored in the paucity of practice MCQ books for the new-style examination. This book, then, was conceived to fill this gap until such time as trainees and other authors have built up their own banks of questions.

Another development that has occurred is the publication of the new curriculum and reading list by the Royal College of Psychiatrists. We have had the benefit of these documents being available during the latter stages of the preparation of this book and have attempted to compose MCQs from appropriate sources with these documents in mind. Other changes around the corner will be the introduction of extended matching items (EMIs) as part of the papers from 2003, and the gradual introduction of criterion referencing into the marking scheme. The latter is a significant and welcome development. Presently, the peer-referenced system ensures that a given proportion only will pass each time, potentially penalising able candidates if a good cohort sits the examination. Criterion referencing involves a number of examiners sitting in front of a given paper and deciding what mark the 'minimally competent candidate' would get. This mark then becomes the pass mark for the examination. It is unlikely that the pass rates will change dramatically when criterion referencing is introduced, but it can reassure candidates who generally prefer to focus on what tasks they have to accomplish on an individual level, rather than worrying about what other candidates are getting up to.

In writing the MCQs contained in this book, we were conscious of a number of needs. The first, to which we have already alluded, is to provide a text that sets out the style of question and format that candidates may encounter on sitting the individual statement papers for the MRCPsych Part II examination. To this end we have attempted to cover both the clinical topics paper and the basic sciences paper, giving three complete papers of each (1200 individual statements in total). A second need is for an individual candidate to be able to test himself or herself under examination-style conditions to get an indication of how he/she will do in the examination. We urge readers to do this since the new-style examination is quite time-pressured: one should not experience this for the first time on the day. A third need, however, is for a text to highlight areas in which one is competent and areas where deficiencies lie. If a reader were to score 100% on every test in this book, while it may boost his/her ego to an enormous degree, it will have benefited the reader little overall since nothing new has been learned. One should be absolutely delighted to get an individual statement wrong, since one will potentially learn so many things: why one was wrong, what things one does not know, what is right, and so on.

Thus, there is a degree of overlap between the first and third needs above, but also some areas of divergence. A series of questions that are only moderately difficult can put the reader at ease, boost ego strength and give a moderate indication of how well one is progressing, given that a number of MCQs in the examination, particularly the clinical topics paper, are relatively straightforward. On the other hand, given that the examination can be very difficult at times, especially the basic sciences paper, and since the marking is still peer-referenced as yet, the only safe way to prepare for the examination is to over-prepare. Difficult MCQs, while sometimes depressing, continually challenge one's sense of security in examination preparation and can stimulate us to do extra: we can always study and improve a little bit more. One should aim not to be the 'minimally competent candidate', since it is not an especially attractive title, and since it is difficult to decide before the examination the minimal volume of knowledge that is compatible with passing.

In writing this book, we have tried to address some of these needs. We have tried to give a mix of representative questions covering the new curriculum in the format and proportions of the most recent Royal College guidelines. By having four authors, we hope that the questions in this book will give a better feel for the differing styles of questioning that one can encounter. We have also attempted to have questions with a range of difficulty so that areas where further study should be directed can be identified from the answers. Most answers in this book contain some short explanatory notes. We have drawn up questions based on our readings of a variety of texts. Almost to a text, the books listed in the references section are heartily recommended by us for MRCPsych preparation. Any specific answers are, however, of marginal interest. If you get an answer right, and know why you were right – move on. If you get an answer wrong, however, you have the opportunity of improving your knowledge base. To assist with this, each answer has a specific reference of the format: **[BC. p345]**. This indicates that information regarding that topic may be found on page 345 of the text listed as 'BC.' in the reference list section. We strongly recommend that you check any areas of uncertainty in these books.

Finally, while we have taken considerable effort to try to check and re-check the accuracy of the various individual statements and answers, it is inevitable that a number of errors may have crept in. If you come across any, please send us a quick note, giving the question number and the inaccuracy, to: mcqs@eircom.net. Allow us to wish you every success in your examinations!

B.R.

M.R.

D.B.

S.G.

Co. Galway, 2002

Acknowledgements

While it is probably foolish to try to thank all who have assisted us with the preparation of this book in some shape or form, since we will undoubtedly forget and offend many, we cannot let the opportunity pass to express our appreciation to the following:

- Our colleagues and other staff in our workplaces for the numerous examples of support they have given us over the years. The encouragement, advice and feedback they have given us on this book, and our previous book for the MRCPsych Part I, have been invaluable.
- Our fellow trainees who have provided an excellent learning environment over the years and much interpersonal support.
- We would like to thank the clinical tutors and other consultants of the Western Health Board Postgraduate Psychiatric Training Scheme who have given us all much in terms of training and unfailing personal support. We would like to acknowledge the contribution to our training made by the following over the years: Dr O. Bradley, Dr C. P. Byrne, Dr P. A. Carney, Dr A. Carroll, Dr J. F. Connolly, Dr E. Corcoran, Dr F. Creaven, Dr A. Cullen, Dr M. Delaney-Warner, Dr J. Dennehy, Prof. T. J. Fahy, Dr C. Hennelly, Dr A. Jeffers, Dr E. Macken, Dr L. Mannion, Dr M. McGuire, Dr M. P. Spellman, Dr P. Noone, Dr D. O'Rourke, Dr R. O'Toole, Dr K. Power, Dr C. Smith, Dr M. Smith.
- To the Professors and other staff of the Institute of Mental Health, Madras Medical College, Chennai, and the Government Stanley Medical College and Hospital, Chennai (Madras).
- To Dr K. M. Malone, Mater Misericordiae Hospital and all of those working on the Ireland North/South Urban/Rural Epidemiological (INSURE) Collaborative Project on the Clinical and Biological Correlates of Suicidal Behaviour.
- Finally to our families and friends who have always provided such support. While our combined extended families comprise a

multitude, we would like to thank a few in a particular: **BR:** Selvaprabha Bangaru-Raju, Dhivyashree, and Deepasree. **MR:** Samantha Fox-Reilly; the Reilly clan: Eileen, Elizabeth, John and Daniel; the Fox clan: Sheila, Jennifer, Rodney and Pat (R.I.P.). **DB:** I would like to thank my parents, Flan and Miriam, Jennifer and Anne and their respective partners. I would like to express my gratitude especially to Jane for her support during my absence while writing the book. Last, and by no means least, "Go raibh maith agaibh go léir" to the Daly family. **SG:** Seán, John, Ann and Nigel.

Question Papers

Question Paper 1: Clinical Topics

1.1 According to the St. Louis' description, Briquet's syndrome can occur in males in exceptional situations only.

1.2 Confabulation is associated with the post-traumatic confusional state.

1.3 According to the Mental Health Act 1983, sections of prisons can be used as hospitals.

1.4 Non-pharmacological treatments for panic disorder include interoceptive exposure.

1.5 Consumption of the pica substance does not reduce the desire for food.

1.6 In individuals with intelligence quotients (I.Q.s) less than 50, males tend to outnumber females at all ages.

1.7 *Diogenes syndrome* (senile self-neglect) occurs less often in men.

1.8 *Psychoanalysis and feminism* was written by Karen Horney.

1.9 Cumming and Henry argued that 'disengagement' has been forced on the elderly through ageist attitudes.

1.10 Sydenham's chorea is associated with obsessive-compulsive symptoms and has a higher incidence in females.

1.11 Drowning is not a common method of suicide among young people.

1.12 Under the Care Programme Approach, the care plan is generally drafted at a meeting of all professionals involved.

1.13 Growth hormone and prolactin secretions are affected in a dose related manner by nicotine.

1.14 In individuals with severe learning difficulty, self-injurious behaviour has a peak occurrence between the ages of 15 to 20.

1.15 The jealous subtype of delusional disorder has a worse outcome than any other subtype.

1.16 Ten per cent of children will have isolated tics in the primary school years.

1.17 The concordance rate for criminality is six times greater in monozygotic twins than in dizygotic twins.

1.18   In designing a study to investigate levels of depressive symptoms in a retirement home, the *Montgomery-Åsberg Depression Rating Scale* (MADRS) may be a more appropriate scale to use than the *Hamilton Rating Scale for Depression: 24 items* (HAM-D 24).

1.19   Musical hallucinations in the hearing impaired are the auditory equivalent of Charles-Bonnet syndrome.

1.20   In mild organic states there is frequently an underestimation of time span.

1.21   Perseveration, impaired serial order behaviour and impersistence occur as a result of a medial frontal lobe lesion.

1.22   In the diagnosis of childhood psychiatric disorders, most syndromes in ICD-10 do not require impairment of social functioning to be present for diagnosis.

1.23   After drinking alcohol, levels of prolactin are lower in individuals with a family history of alcoholism than in controls.

1.24   It has been found in epidemiological surveys of obsessive-compulsive disorder that checking rituals are more common in women.

1.25   In ICD-10 behavioural impairment associated with learning disability can only be specified as a fourth character in the standard diagnostic code.

1.26   A study of clinicians diagnosing attention-deficit disorder using DSM-III criteria found that κ scores obtained generally were greater than 0.70.

1.27   In homicides within families matricide is the commonest form.

1.28   The Mini-Mental State Examination (MMSE) is not particularly useful for detecting nominal dysphasias.

1.29   Seating arrangements are used to facilitate changes in system-based family therapy.

1.30   Self-injurious behaviour is pronounced in syndromes such as Prader-Willi syndrome.

1.31   In Huntington's disease with childhood onset, muscular rigidity and tremor are more common than choreiform movements.

1.32   In 1992, a World Health Organization study found that the incidence of schizophrenia was similar in ten different countries.

1.33   Binge eating disorder has an increased incidence of binging episodes than does bulimia nervosa.

1.34   The automatisms associated with frontal lobe seizures tend to be shorter in duration than those arising from temporal lobe seizures.

1.35 The most common visual hallucinations in Charles Bonnet syndrome are human form simple hallucinations.

1.36 The risk of puerperal relapse in bipolar affective disorder is thought to be especially high if the disorder has been predominantly depressive in nature.

1.37 There are decreased levels of social harm in a society where a less episodic pattern of drinking predominates

1.38 In risk assessment, a patient with schizophrenia who reports that he recognises the identity of the person who is speaking the command hallucinations he hears, is more likely to act out on the command hallucinations.

1.39 An electroencephalogram recorded under hypnosis showing decreased alpha activity and increased theta and delta activity in a healthy sixty five year old is normal.

1.40 Robert Spitzer was the main architect of DSM-III introduced in 1980.

1.41 A depressed skull fracture does not significantly increase the risk of post-traumatic epilepsy.

1.42 In the diagnosis of childhood psychiatric disorders, both DSM-IV and ICD-10 have multiaxial frameworks in which general medical conditions are listed on axis III.

1.43 Patients with Korsakoff's syndrome are capable of new learning.

1.44 With regard to William's syndrome, those in whom the gene deletion is paternally derived have shorter stature than those in whom the deletion is maternally derived.

1.45 Children of indulging parents commonly lack self-reliance and self-concept more than the children of authoritative parents.

1.46 Hysterical pseudocyesis is associated with hyperschemazia.

1.47 Final outcome in specific retardation may be as related to co-morbid conduct disorder as to specific reading disorder.

1.48 Freud regarded *déjà vu* as being associated with the recall of unconscious fantasies.

1.49 When compared to older children, younger children show less amnesia to traumatic events.

1.50 Among adolescents, girls and boys have equal prevalence of psychiatric disorders since girls have higher rates of internalising problems while boys have higher rates of behaviour problems.

1.51 In opiate drug abusers heroin overdose is easier to manage than a methadone overdose.

1.52 The term *compensation neurosis* was first used by Miller in 1961 during his work as a neurologist with an insurance company.

1.53 In a doctor-patient relationship confidentiality is the patient's right.

1.54 Affecting about 3% of children, night terrors typically involve a frightened expression with the child lying on his back in bed moaning or screaming.

1.55 In studying social factors in the elderly, retirement itself is not a cause of increased morbidity.

1.56 With regard to genetic studies, a linkage with the chromosomal locus Xq28 has been reported as a determinant of homosexual behaviour.

1.57 Among individuals who develop a significant mental illness, the rate of conviction for violent offences is increased more in females than males over their baseline rates.

1.58 In the behavioural treatment of childhood behavioural disorders, *over-correction* is seen as a counter-productive response often leading to a paradoxical increase in the behaviour.

1.59 Fragile X (E) Syndrome (FRAXE) is associated with GCC triplet expansions and shows anticipation.

1.60 The fact that suicide rates are higher in the Spring and Summer months is a trend that is common to countries in both the northern and southern hemispheres.

1.61 Lobar atrophy is a recognised, but not characteristic, feature of Pick's disease.

1.62 William's syndrome is associated with hyponatraemia.

1.63 Females affected with fragile X syndrome show the following features: tangential speech, executive function difficulties and poor verbal memory.

1.64 Spastic quadriplegia is believed to be the only type of cerebral palsy associated with an acute interruption of oxygen supply.

1.65 Pharmacodynamic tolerance of alcohol does not refer to the adaptation of liver cells to metabolise alcohol more rapidly.

1.66 In both DSM-IV and ICD-10, Rett's syndrome is included under the pervasive developmental disorders.

1.67 Although Jung considered psychological illness an individual experience, he recognise the benefits of group therapy.

1.68 In 1992, the Royal College of Psychiatrists recommended 8 medium-stay adult inpatient beds per 100,000 population.

1.69 Counting rituals are more common in pure obsessive-compulsive disorder (OCD) than in co-morbid Tourette's disorder and OCD.

1.70 An absence of euphoria does not differentiate a delirious state from a manic state in the elderly.

1.71 *Dermatitis artefacta* may precede the onset of a psychotic illness.

1.72 The mortality rate rises when women drink more than 2 units of alcohol per day.

1.73 The term *somatoform disorder* was newly introduced in DSM-IV.

1.74 Caffeine dependence may be diagnosed under DSM-IV.

1.75 A Scandinavian study of suicide in schizophrenia found that most suicides were planned in advance.

1.76 In Great Britain, residential care accounts for 50% of the total direct cost of schizophrenia per year.

1.77 Self-view as a victim is significantly associated with dangerousness to others.

1.78 Rutter *et al.* found that, in contrast to rates of psychiatric disorder, the prevalence of specific reading retardation was equal in an inner-London area and in the Isle of Wight among 10-year-olds.

1.79 In transient tic disorder, transient phonic tics can occur in the absence of motor tics.

1.80 One of the changes occurring in derealisation as described by Lewis includes loss of the ability to recall images with vividness.

1.81 Following head injury, receptive language recovery predates expressive language recovery.

1.82 Around one third of individuals who have been stalked by another person have been found to meet criteria for post-traumatic stress disorder.

1.83 *Solution focused therapy* is a variant of the structural approach in family therapy.

1.84 The prototypical case of Munchausen's syndrome is an itinerant male.

1.85 In normal individuals, the most frequent number of repeats of the CGG trinucleotide repeat sequence in the FMR_1 gene is 30.

1.86 On switching a patient with schizophrenia from an oral antipsychotic to a depot antipsychotic, one should aim to do this gradually over four weeks.

1.87 Obsessive-compulsive disorder differs from other anxiety disorders in that it is more common in old age.

1.88 The McNaughten rules were established to form a yardstick for the definition of diminished responsibility in the context of crime.

1.89 Atlanto-axial instability is a recognised feature of Down's syndrome.

1.90 Kandel proposed a four-stage model of substance misuse in adolescents.

1.91 In object relation theory, the original object for a neonate is the mother.

1.92 The schizodepressive subtype of schizoaffective disorder is biologically more related to schizophrenia than to affective disorder.

1.93 The most common cause of death for infants below one year of age is sudden infant death syndrome (SIDS).

1.94 As with younger patients, in the elderly patient with depression the presence of anxiety in the clinical presentation is thought to be predictive of good response to electroconvulsive therapy.

1.95 Neuroimaging studies can distinguish fronto-temporal dementia from Alzheimer's dementia.

1.96 One of the cognitive deficits identified in obsessive-compulsive disorder is the inability to be distracted by other competing stimuli.

1.97 Behavioural analysis of arson commonly does not identify contributory factors.

1.98 Family therapy for anorexia nervosa is more beneficial for most patients than individual therapy in preventing relapse.

1.99 The specificity of carbohydrate deficient transferrin in the diagnosis of alcohol misuse is lower in women than in men.

1.100 In DSM-IV, though paraphilias and gender identity disorders are grouped under disorders of adult personality and behaviour, sexual dysfunctions are not.

1.101 Retirement does not have significant effect on subsequent quality of life.

1.102 In patients who have been prescribed a long-acting benzodiazepine and who have been taking this in normal doses for between 3 to 12 months, the proportion that will develop a discontinuation syndrome is in the region of 10–20%.

1.103 40% of three-year-olds with specific language delay have behavioural problems.

1.104 Auditory hallucinations of sounds other than voices have little diagnostic value in schizophrenia.

1.105 The exhibitionist may go on exposing to the victim if he elicits the desired response.

1.106 Unlike muscle relaxation, massed practice has not been found to be of use in the treatment of Tourette's syndrome in adolescents.

1.107 The electroencephalogram (EEG) findings in patients with Alzheimer's disease are similar to those of multi-infarct dementia.

1.108 In individuals with frequent self-injurious behaviour, β-endorphin levels are often higher than in controls.

1.109 Three of the four vulnerability factors described by Brown and Harris are of key importance in attachment theory.

1.110 A reduced propensity for aggressiveness is associated with encephalitis.

1.111 Assessments of self-harm by non-medical staff with adequate training are as satisfactory as those performed by psychiatrists.

1.112 After onset, the average proportion of lifetime spent ill has been estimated at 20% for both bipolar and unipolar patients.

1.113 Post mortem studies of non-specific frontal lobe dementia have reported Pick cells.

1.114 The risk of a child exhibiting conduct disorder is doubled if the child comes from a large family.

1.115 The Lancaster electrode placement position for electroconvulsive therapy is recommended over the d'Elia electrode placement by the Royal College of Psychiatrists.

1.116 The rule of a diagnostic hierarchy is that any given diagnosis excludes a diagnosis lower down in the hierarchy but may include those that are higher up.

1.117 Post-menopausal women are usually benefited by moderate consumption of alcohol.

1.118 The incidence of alcoholism tends to be lower in societies where children are exposed when young to alcohol in the settings of strong family groups.

1.119 The main indications for electroconvulsive therapy in the elderly are avolition and thought content disturbances.

1.120 Unresolved anger turned inward is the core characteristic of Engel's psychodynamic *pain-prone patient* concept.

1.121 Sheie's syndrome is a recessive lysosomal storage disease.

1.122 Alcohol abuse by the abused spouse is associated with the physical abuse.

1.123 In Prader-Willi syndrome, whether it is produced by microdeletion or uniparental disomy, the facial characteristics are similar.

1.124 June Singer agreed with Jung's view that the early embryo is bisexual in her book *Androgyny: the Opposites Within*.

1.125 Total sleep deprivation has long-lasting effects on depression in contrast to the phase advance of sleep cycle.

1.126 In legal terms, rape can occur even if consent is given by a mentally competent adult.

1.127 The Hayflick Limit states that human diploid cells cultured in vivo have a finite lifespan.

1.128 In a patient with suicidal ideas, the fact that the patient is an Indian female would be associated with an increased risk.

1.129 Gerstman's syndrome includes agnosia, apraxia, aphasia and acalculia.

1.130 At diagnosis, about 30% of individuals with human immuno-deficiency virus infection have suicidal ideation.

1.131 All of Freud's case reports were from patients under fifty years of age.

1.132 The *abstinence violation effect* refers to the pragmatic approach that accepts that some people will continue to use illicit drugs.

1.133 The majority of patients with selective mutism do not make significant recovery with treatment.

1.134 Among psychiatric inpatients, narcissistic personality disorder is seen more frequently than paranoid personality disorder.

1.135 In group psychotherapy for bereavement in people with learning disabilities, three therapists has been recommended as the ideal number for the work.

1.136 Monosomy X in spontaneous abortions has been shown to be associated with increased maternal age.

1.137 Severe morbid onychophagia is commonly associated with cranio-mandibular dysfunction.

1.138 Loosening of associations is less common in late-onset schizophrenia.

1.139 Freud in *Totem and Taboo* (1913) proposed that the totem symbolises the primal father who was murdered when his sons rebelled against his mastery of the primal horde.

1.140 Social cognitive products refer to a form of problem-solving training where role-play and modelling are used in combination with cognitive strategies.

1.141 In a lawsuit brought by a patient against a doctor, the patient can bar certain embarrassing issues from the doctor's testimony.

1.142 A positive family history of affective disorders has been suggested to be a predictor of good response to carbamazepine in bipolar affective disorder.

1.143 Neuroacanthocytosis can present with symptoms similar to that of Huntington's disease.

1.144 There is an unusually high incidence of attention deficit hyperactivity disorder in Japan.

1.145 A patient saying 'deat' for 'beat' is exhibiting phonemic paraphasia.

1.146 An exhibitionist will tend to expose himself in many different locations in order to try to make detection by the police more difficult.

1.147 Anxiety disorders are more prevalent than mood disorders in learning disabled people presenting with self-injurious behaviour.

1.148 In *folie à deux*, a psychodynamic interpretation of the relationship between the two people involved would tend to reveal homosexual feelings.

1.149 Lesions in the left temperoparieto-occipital junction characteristically produce an impaired ability for repetition.

1.150 In family situations where a parent has major depression, the proportion of offspring who will develop a psychiatric condition in childhood or adolescence is estimated to be 60%.

1.151 In psychotherapy with elderly patients, during the early stages of therapy transference and the countertransference are likely to be reversed.

1.152 Transsexuals are usually convinced of being the wrong sex by the age of eight.

1.153 Conduct disorder is ten times more common in male adolescents than in female adolescents.

1.154 In the treatment of temazepam dependence, when switching from this agent to diazepam one should bear in mind that roughly 2 mg of temazepam is equivalent to 1 mg of diazepam.

1.155 In Gilles de la Tourette syndrome, opioid peptides have been directly implicated in its pathophysiology.

1.156 *Counter-regulation* is employed as a psychological explanation of anorexia nervosa.

1.157 Among patients with personality disorders, those with dissocial personality disorder most commonly bring *false imprisonment* allegations.

1.158 The proportion of individuals who develop a manic episode in old age who have not had a previous history of depression is about 5%.

1.159 The hypothesis that the mind can be meaningfully separated from the body is called mind-body dualism.

1.160 Dramatisation in dreams is typically concrete.

1.161 Reduced electroencephalogram (EEG) alpha activity in alcoholics is a state biological marker.

1.162 The term *mongolism* was derived from the classification system of learning difficulties proposed by J. Langdon Down.

1.163 The commonest cause of Prader-Willi Syndrome is uniparental disomy.

1.164 The Beckwith-Wiedemann syndrome involves a deletion on the long arm of chromosome 11.

1.165 With the exception of simple schizophrenia, the subtypes of schizophrenia are valid clinical entities.

1.166 The prevalence of depressive episodes is lower in single females than in married females.

1.167 In patients with agenesis of the corpus callosum, clinical findings when present are not related to the agenesis.

1.168 In individuals with hypothyroidism, it has been shown that the use of tricyclic antidepressants may induce rapid cycling bipolar disorder.

1.169 In cannabis intoxication, the degree of driving impairment can be predicted reliably by measuring blood levels of cannabis.

1.170 *Family-based conduct disorder* is associated with marked disturbances in interactions and behaviour between the child and child's family with significant others in the child's life (for example teachers).

1.171 Acute dystonia occurs more commonly in younger patients.

1.172 Hypochondriasis may be viewed psychodynamically as a derivative of aggressive or oral drives.

1.173 Independent women with high hostility have a raised rate of depression over independent women with moderate hostility.

1.174 Harsh discipline in childhood is associated with higher rates of anxiety but lower rates of offending in later life.

1.175 Self-reported family difficulties tend to remit with the patient's clinical recovery.

1.176 In offenders with schizophrenia, delusions of paranormal content are more closely related to violence than are persecutory delusions.

1.177 Maple syrup urine disease can be controlled by a synthetic diet lacking in branched chain amino acids.

1.178 According to Jungian analysts, there is a marked change in the proportion of animus and anima in the individual when he/she enters later life.

1.179 In anorexia nervosa, pelvic ultrasound is a useful tool in measuring progress following treatment.

1.180 In his concept of *depressive spectrum disease*, Winokur asserts that borderline personality disorder and alcoholism form part of a spectrum with depression.

1.181 To find a person guilty of the *actus reus*, there is no need for him to have had the *mens rea* for that crime.

1.182 The prevalence of obesity in individuals with Prader-Willi syndrome is about 80%.

1.183 Erikson's *Industry versus Inferiority* corresponds to the latency stage in Freud's theory of development.

1.184 With regard to late-onset Alzheimer's disease, it is found that one in four individuals with the condition have a family history of dementia.

1.185 Differences between the values of old and young may be more pronounced in developed countries than in developing countries.

1.186 General intelligence is retained in children with Landau-Kleffner syndrome.

1.187 Research on recent memory shows that early attachment relationships are internalised and encoded as procedural memory.

1.188 With regard to renal failure, dialysis dementia has become uncommon since the recognition that ammonia contributes to its aetiology.

1.189 The *Mini Mental State Examination* contains tests of information.

1.190 Among drug users who are arrested for acquisitive crime, around 85% will report that they committed the crime to pay for their drugs.

1.191 Stable risk factors identified in stalkers include a history of domestic violence and a criminal record.

1.192 With regard to behavioural therapy for obsessive-compulsive disorder, patients who do not consistently recognise that their beliefs are untrue do less well unless adjunctive pharmacotherapy is also prescribed.

1.193 'Kicking the habit' does not refer to the barbiturate withdrawal state.

1.194 In the families of individuals with an addiction, the concept of *codependence* contains the characteristics of *denial* and *disabling*.

1.195 Patients with first onset of depression in later life have a poorer treatment response and more cognitive impairment.

1.196 In the CDC classification for staging HIV infection, Stage IV B refers to opportunistic infections as defined for AIDS.

1.197 Methadone maintenance is associated with a significant reduction in crime rate.

1.198 In contrast to lithium, in the elderly venlafaxine generally does not need dosage adjustment from doses recommended for younger adults.

1.199 Children admitted to hospital may go through non-sequential phases of protest-despair-detachment during a protracted admission.

1.200 The Louis-Bar syndrome is associated with an IgM deficiency.

Question Paper 2: Clinical Topics

2.1 Decreased hippocampal volume is a common finding in chronic post-traumatic stress disorder.

2.2 Visual perseveration is associated with posterior cerebral artery infarctions.

2.3 Patients suffering with psychotic depression are more likely to complete suicide than those with depression without psychotic features.

2.4 With regard to clinical governance, an *indicator* in quality assurance is a pre-set criterion of good clinical practice.

2.5 In a co-dependency relationship, people living together equally take care of each other at the expense of other social relationships.

2.6 A trial of lithium augmentation for treatment-resistant depression should consist of at least two months' treatment.

2.7 Cumulative incidence is the proportion of subjects who have developed a disease within a specified time period.

2.8 The *care management programme* is not led by health services.

2.9 Patients with mild degrees of all key symptoms of the ICD-10 diagnostic criteria of anorexia nervosa may be best described as having 'atypical anorexia nervosa'.

2.10 While alcohol intake increases the likelihood of sustaining a head injury, it has not been shown to worsen the outcome of the injury.

2.11 The Present State Examination (PSE) was developed as a reliable descriptive instrument for clinical phenomena rather than a diagnostic instrument.

2.12 A paranoid personality has a definite association with onset of later life depression.

2.13 The category of 'Religious or Spiritual Problems' was introduced in DSM-III-R.

2.14 Hyperventilation induces panic symptoms in around 60% of patients with panic disorder.

2.15 The human immunodeficiency virus, simian immunodeficiency virus, and the visna virus are all lentiviruses.

2.16 In Kuf's disease, the inborn error of metabolism results in glucocerebrosides being deposited in the brain.

2.17 Beck's cognitive triad of depression are: a negative view of self, a negative view of others and a negative view of the future.

2.18 In contrast to generalised anxiety disorder, patients with panic disorder who have been treated previously with benzodiazepines tend to respond less well to buspirone.

2.19 The following symptoms and signs are useful in diagnosing depression in the medically ill: pessimism, feelings of helplessness and depressed appearance.

2.20 Carbamazepine may be more efficacious than lithium in the depressive subtype of schizoaffective disorder while of equal efficacy in the bipolar subtype.

2.21 Depression in schizophrenia shows a two-peak occurrence: one in the acute phase and the other in the chronic negative stage.

2.22 After stroke, the commonest effect on sexual functioning is a diminished libido despite normal physical functioning.

2.23 A British study of patients post-mastectomy found that just 25% develop psychiatric morbidity.

2.24 None of the transmissible spongiform encephalopathies induce an immune response.

2.25 A hyperdopaminergic state is not a recognised feature of mania.

2.26 The states of delirium that occur in nicotinic acid deficiency and Wernicke's disease are similar in clinical presentation.

2.27 Schilder's disease (diffuse cerebral sclerosis) causes psychotic symptoms that are indistinguishable from schizophrenia.

2.28 On average, patients with schizophrenia living in homes with low expressed emotion relapse once every three years.

2.29 The high suicide rate among young men in rural China compared to other countries has been linked to fewer psychiatric services being available.

2.30 While both validation therapy and resolution therapy search for meaning behind the confused communication of the elderly with dementia, the former seeks for the meanings in past events while the latter seeks them in the present.

2.31 Bilateral high-dose electroconvulsive therapy three times per week for the emergency treatment of depression gives the fastest response with fewer cognitive side-effects.

2.32 A disorder of sexual preference where sexual arousal is obtained through photographing others engaged in intercourse is known as scoptophilia.

2.33 Paranoid traits are approximately 40% heritable.

2.34 The reduction of suicide rates attributed to the introduction of the less toxic natural gas in Great Britain in the 1960s was most marked among the elderly.

2.35 In *Principal Component Analysis*, components can be rotated using Varimax to achieve more satisfactory solutions.

2.36 A significant relationship has been found between the birth of a female child and the development of puerperal psychosis.

2.37 Prior severity of dependence in alcoholics is unlikely to predict future relapse but is more likely to predict the severity of relapse.

2.38 Enuresis tends to occur in stages 1 and 2 of non-rapid eye movement (NREM) sleep.

2.39 In neuroleptic malignant syndrome (NMS), bromocriptine is used for the treatment of autonomic instability and hyperthermia.

2.40 In individuals with schizophrenia a decreased rate of blinking is seen.

2.41 *Boufée delireante* does not fulfil the ICD-10 diagnostic criteria of schizophrenia.

2.42 Neither DSM-IV nor ICD-10 has a separate category for puerperal disorders.

2.43 Follow up studies of suicide in major affective disorder have shown the following are risk factors for suicide after one year: parasuicide, hopelessness and alcohol misuse.

2.44 *Hyperaesthetic jealousy* is synonymous with *projected jealousy*.

2.45 In Fahr's disease, intellectual impairment is a result of subcortical calcification.

2.46 The incidence of problem alcohol use in individuals over the age of 85 is negligible.

2.47 In frontal lobe dementia histological changes include spongiform changes.

2.48 The majority of women who commit infanticide have a mental illness at the time of the offence.

2.49 Delirium itself contributes significantly to six-month mortality.

2.50 The *Clifton Assessment Procedures for the Elderly* contains a behavioural rating scale that comprises four elements: physical disability, apraxia, communication difficulties and social disturbance.

2.51 Women with a history of bipolar affective disorder have a one-in-two risk of puerperal relapse.

2.52 The principal cause of death in suicidal hanging is fracture-dislocation of the second cervical vertebra with severance of the spinal cord.

2.53 To make a diagnosis of post-schizophrenic depression, ICD-10 does not require that some positive symptoms of schizophrenia still remain with depressive symptoms.

2.54 In medical wards, the prevalence of elderly patients who are delirious is in the region of 4–8%.

2.55 Psychological treatments in the elderly have similar efficacy to those used in younger patients.

2.56 The risk of developing Alzheimer's Disease is increased three-fold for homozygotes carrying the ε4 allele of the apolipoprotein E gene.

2.57 30% of elderly delirious in-patients have depression.

2.58 First-degree relatives of individuals with alcohol dependence have increased static ataxia.

2.59 The premorbid state and the setting of drug taking are significant factors in determining the reaction to the acute ingestion of cannabis.

2.60 Diurnal enuresis is more common among young boys.

2.61 ICD-10 and DSM-IV do not give equal weight to the presence of functional impairment in diagnosing schizophrenia.

2.62 In the elderly, the proportion of patients who have an ICD-10 diagnosis of generalised anxiety disorder and a comorbid depressive episode is about 20–30%.

2.63 The *Geriatric Depression Scale* does not retain its validity in the physically ill elderly.

2.64 Awareness of the existence of activity of the self is characteristically not affected in schizophrenia.

2.65 Increased social activity is considered to be directly proportional to increased suicidal rate.

2.66 Mouth ulceration is a recognised feature of the tobacco withdrawal state.

2.67 The commonest neoplasm in patients with the human immunodeficiency virus (HIV) is Hodgkin's lymphoma.

2.68 It has been shown that a correlation between anxiety symptoms and negative life events only holds true for individuals who perceive an external locus of control.

2.69 Schizophrenia has been reported to have a four times lower risk of suicide than the personality disorders.

2.70 The gene that has been found to be responsible for the transmission of early-onset autosomal dominant familial Alzheimer's disease in the Volga German family line is the *S182* gene on chromosome 14.

2.71 Of children born to human immunodeficiency (HIV) positive mothers that develop cognitive and motor disabilities, about a quarter develop a progressive encephalopathy with an invariably fatal outcome.

2.72 It has not been shown that spontaneous elaboration is a neuropsychological trait impaired specifically in depressive pseudodementia.

2.73 Endogenous pentapeptides bind with μ-opioid receptors.

2.74 In patients who develop late-onset persecutory delusional symptoms, the commonest emotional response is depressed mood.

2.75 Side-effects of desmopression (synthetic vasopeptide) include: rhinitis, conjunctivitis, nasal pain and congestion.

2.76 Delusions are more common in vascular dementia than in Alzheimer's disease.

2.77 *Per capita*, the inhabitants of the Republic of Ireland are not the greatest consumers of alcohol in the world.

2.78 Increased production of dynorphin is associated with chronic amphetamine use.

2.79 Most children are able to read single short words by the age of six years.

2.80 In a primary care survey it was found that patients who scored highly for hypochondriasis rated their mothers as more caring than low scorers.

2.81 Left occipital lobe lesions cause anomia, colour agnosia and contralateral achromatopsia.

2.82 In the debate about how well diagnostic criteria for psychiatric syndromes developed for use in adult populations can be used for children, obsessive-compulsive disorder is one of the most commonly cited examples to highlight potential difficulties.

2.83 *Gerstmann-Sträussler syndrome*, a transmissible spongiform encephalopathy, is inherited in families as an autosomal recessive condition.

2.84 It has been estimated that one third of female alcoholic patients have a history of an eating disorder.

2.85   Simple advice, when given by any doctor and only by a suitably trained nurse, is associated with a significant decline in hazardous drinking.

2.86   The *Addiction Severity Index* is a self-report questionnaire that has established reasonable reliability and may be used with abusers of alcohol or other psychoactive substances.

2.87   Under English law a very intoxicated person cannot be held to have committed a crime requiring *mens rea*.

2.88   Jung stated that individuals with histrionic personality disorder were of an extroverted intuitive type.

2.89   Naltrexone worsens the attention disturbances in Tourette's disorder.

2.90   A number of studies have established that the level of alcohol dependence is the best predictor of whether controlled drinking in the future might be sustainable for a given patient.

2.91   Children diagnosed with attention deficit hyperactivity disorder that present with predominant conduct symptoms can be given a dual diagnosis using DSM-IV.

2.92   Benedict Augustin Morel developed the concept of degenerate heredity.

2.93   In Huntington's disease, behavioural disturbances commonly predate the onset of neurological symptoms.

2.94   Motivational interviewing the patient with an addiction will often require forceful challenging of the patient's perceptions of his/her past behaviours and an ability to deal with the arguments that can sometimes develop from this.

2.95   In the treatment of torture victims, the *testimony method* is a therapy in which the central part of therapy is the retelling of the trauma.

2.96   Freud's last publications included *The Future of an Illusion* and *Civilisation and Narcissism*.

2.97   According to Baron-Cohen and Hobson, the primary deficit in autism is language acquisition defects.

2.98   In the psychometric assessment of children, the British Ability Scales not only test perceptual matching but also memory.

2.99   Among residents in social service secure units, young people with learning disabilities have a greater number of placements outside the home than their peers without learning disability.

2.100 With regard to group psychotherapy, Yalom felt that universality must be linked to insight in order to be helpful.

2.101 Around 25% of children in developed countries suffer from obesity.

2.102 In amphetamine-induced psychosis, paranoid delusions are much more common than hallucinations.

2.103 Factors associated with challenging behaviour in people with learning disability include: pain, epilepsy, Lesch-Nyhan syndrome and sedative anticonvulsant medication.

2.104 In *literal paraphasia* the individual cannot find the correct word but can still make his meaning clear.

2.105 In countries where there is the highest *per capita* income, the elderly have lowest economic participation.

2.106 The proportion of children with autism who do not develop useful speech is about half.

2.107 The course of blepharospasm that occurs in elderly is often protracted and constant over many years.

2.108 The fact that somatic complaints are rare in Alzheimer's dementia helps distinguish it clinically from vascular dementia.

2.109 3% of secondary school students are solvent abusers.

2.110 The occurrence of biological symptoms differentiates depression in middle childhood from depression in adolescence.

2.111 Baldness does not increase the seizure threshold in patients receiving electroconvulsive therapy.

2.112 The inability to name parts of one's body after, for example, a cerebrovascular event, is known as the *coenestopathic state*.

2.113 Patients with schizophrenia relatively frequently act violently on command hallucinations.

2.114 The most commonly quoted prevalence of mental retardation is approximately 1%.

2.115 Children, whether they are in the mild or severe mental retardation ranges, share common psychiatric disorders, including emotional, conduct, and hyperactivity disorders.

2.116 With regard to the giving of information a *patient-based* standard exists where a doctor must give the level of information necessary to allow the patient to operate his or her autonomy.

2.117 In European countries, the elderly tend to be more alone than lonely.

2.118 In Great Britain, among those who got married in the 1990s, about

25% of these marriages will end in divorce.

2.119 For adults, and to a lesser extent for children, mild learning disability is always socially determined.

2.120 The Mental Health Act (1945) of the Republic of Ireland does not provide for the direct diversion of a psychiatrically unwell offender from the court to hospital.

2.121 Mental retardation does not refer only to substantial limitation in present functioning.

2.122 Researchers have used trisomy 16 mice as a potential Down syndrome model.

2.123 Research has shown that *reality orientation* and *validation therapy*, two psychological therapies, are effective in encouraging orientation in the elderly.

2.124 The clinical sign of walking with small steps is not useful in reliably distinguishing the gait disturbance of Parkinson's disease from the gait disturbances sometimes seen in multi-infarct disease.

2.125 Lewy body dementia does not generally show cortical neuritic senile plaques.

2.126 With regard to the continuity of obsessive-compulsive disorder from childhood to adulthood, the continuity of the syndrome is stronger than the continuity of obsessive-compulsive symptoms.

2.127 The Geriatric Depression Scale (GDS) and the Cornell Scale have been developed to assess depression in the general population of elderly.

2.128 Evidence based medicine is least helpful in prescribing psychotropic medications for people with learning disability.

2.129 70% of patients with Parkinson's disease show depressive symptoms.

2.130 Family therapy is generally quite useful even if both parents are undergoing divorce proceedings.

2.131 Psychoanalysis concepts describe *regression* often occurring to a particular point of fixation.

2.132 System theorists base their thinking on the work of cybernetics.

2.133 DSM-IV describes adaptive functioning as a mixture of: social interpersonal skills, functional academic skills and occupational skills.

2.134 In fragile X syndrome, the range of clinical expression of the syndrome is related to the degree to which the *FMR*-1 gene is methylated.

2.135 Age related changes that may affect drug handling include decreased gastric emptying and decreased pH.

2.136 It is common for only one child in a family to be abused.

2.137 Tuberous sclerosis is the third most common neuro-cutaneous syndrome.

2.138 When a psychiatrist interviews a patient in a forensic setting, issues of prognosis are usually of lesser importance than in the clinical setting.

2.139 Al-Ateen is a support group which uses the '12 Step' programme for teenage alcoholics.

2.140 *Existentialism* is a philosophical theory that gives priority to causation over phenomenology and ontology.

2.141 In Sturge-Weber syndrome, computerised tomography (CT) scan findings cannot be bettered by magnetic resonance imaging (MRI) findings.

2.142 Sexual offences comprise about 5% of all offences.

2.143 Studies of outpatient treatment with *dialectical behaviour therapy* in personality-disordered patients have shown relatively poor long-term outcomes.

2.144 20% of patients with Down's syndrome experience episodes of depressive illness during their lives.

2.145 Alertness is not disturbed in dementia of moderate severity.

2.146 DSM-IV differs from ICD-10 in its classification in that it specifies an I.Q. of less than 75 is necessary to diagnose mental retardation, while in ICD-10 the I.Q. must be less than 70.

2.147 Freud described Leonardo da Vinci as a passive homosexual.

2.148 In schizophrenia, hallucinations have been shown to have little effect on violent behaviour.

2.149 Rapid inpatient detoxification of benzodiazepine abuse is not a safe procedure.

2.150 Coerced false confessions are not common in depression.

2.151 Carl Jung thought that the personal unconscious on its own is capable of anticipating the future.

2.152 The ethical principle of autonomy translates legally into 'battery'.

2.153 In DSM-IV, children are required to have depressive symptoms for a minimum of twelve months to make a diagnosis of dysthymic disorder.

2.154 While there are roughly 50 causes of mental retardation linked to the X chromosome, about 40% of mental retardation that is X-linked is caused by fragile X syndrome.

2.155 The amotivational syndrome has been a consistent finding in heavy cannabis users in controlled studies of long-term use.

2.156 Lacan proposed the idea that the unconscious is structured like a language.

2.157 The prevalence of social anxiety in William's syndrome is around 5%.

2.158 Self-injury is a marked part of the behavioural phenotypes of *cri du chat* syndrome, Smith-Magenis syndrome, Angelman syndrome and Cornelia de Lange syndrome.

2.159 In a study of performance in pilots who were regular cannabis users, following a single ingestion of tetrahydrocanabinol they showed impairment of performance for less than twelve hours.

2.160 Castration anxiety refers to the male child's wishes to exclude or destroy the father.

2.161 Body rocking after two years is not abnormal.

2.162 A specific cause can be identified only in about half of individuals with severe mental retardation.

2.163 Under the Misuse of Drugs Act (1971), Class A drugs include: heroin, morphine, pethidine, cocaine, amphetamines and hallucinogens.

2.164 In the 'Dorian Gray' delusion, a patient thinks that others are aging but he remains the same age.

2.165 In children, DSM-IV requires hypomanic symptoms to last for four days to make a clinical diagnosis.

2.166 Extracampine hallucinations may occur in normal individuals.

2.167 The *Neale Analysis of Reading Ability* is a short test of reading speed, accuracy and comprehension.

2.168 The term *narcissistic rage* was used by Kernberg to describe the reactions of persons with narcissistic personality disorder to injuries to their self-esteem.

2.169 Parent-infant psychotherapy was developed by Hopkins.

2.170 The primary prevention strategies for learning difficulties include screening for phenylketonuria.

2.171 Illusions of the pareidolic type are often prodromal in delirium tremens.

2.172 The most common cause of environmental agnosia is cerebrovascular disease.

2.173 Controlled studies concerning the differentiation of agoraphobic patients from other anxious patients along defective parental care dimensions have yielded negative results.

2.174 Moderate learning disability refers to an adult mental age of 6 to 9 years.

2.175 The *Adult Attachment Interview* was developed by Mary Main to test the current attachment between the child and the parent.

2.176 *One-way amnesia* is usual in multiple personality disorder.

2.177 10% of adolescents have been reported to experience episodic amnesia associated with drinking habits.

2.178 In pseudobulbar palsy, emotional disturbances are often unlikely to be mood incongruent.

2.179 Studies in British prisons have shown that major psychotic illness has a higher prevalence in prisoners than in the general population.

2.180 *Perseveration* can be understood as a special kind of *intrusion*.

2.181 Classification of degree of violence in an assault is not a reliable measure of risk assessment.

2.182 Between the ages of 1 to 19, the death rate among mild to moderate learning disability is three times that of the general population.

2.183 In British prisons, the majority of completed prison suicides occur in those prisoners who have a previous history of psychiatric illness.

2.184 There is no firm evidence that carbamazepine is useful in the treatment of aggression in people with learning disability unless there is evidence of an affective component.

2.185 The incidence of intoxication at the time of offence does not differ significantly between female offenders and male offenders.

2.186 Tetrahydrobiopterin deficiency causes a clinical syndrome that is similar to the hyperphenylalaninemia syndrome.

2.187 *Primary ontological security* is a term that is used to describe the existential position of a person with a centrally firm sense of his own and other people's reality and identity.

2.188 Children with retinopathy of prematurity have a very low rate of autism.

2.189 Consumerism has increased the importance of the nonmaleficence principle but it has reduced the beneficence principle of ethics.

2.190 Receptive prosody impairment is a feature of posterior superior left temporal lobe lesions.

2.191 In England and Wales, *Dolci Incapax* describes in law that children under 10 years are partially criminally responsible.

2.192 In Down's Syndrome, the extra chromosome 21 is of paternal origin in approximately one quarter of cases.

2.193 *Tower of babble* refers to the controversies that exist among dispositional personality theorists.

2.194 John Bell's family therapy involves doing all the therapy with the whole family present.

2.195 In fragile X syndrome the *Sherman Paradox* refers to the phenomenon of genetic anticipation.

2.196 In England and Wales, in order for a patient to recover damages from a doctor for the tort of battery, the patient has had to suffer some actual harm.

2.197 Under British law, automatism secondary to epilepsy is not classified as non-insane automatism.

2.198 Matching theory predicts that if a person can perform numerous alternative behaviours, the frequency of each behaviour occurring will be directly proportional to the amount of reinforcement each received.

2.199 In some cases it has been found that a single dose of amphetamine may improve mania.

2.200 Infantile spasms are strongly associated with autistic behaviour.

Question Paper 3: Clinical Topics

3.1 Erections occurring in response to erotic stimuli are not less likely to be androgen sensitive than nocturnal penile tumescence (NPT).

3.2 The decline in cognitive functions seen in a proportion of epileptic patients tends to leave the personality structure relatively intact.

3.3 After a suicide attempt, the proportion of elderly people who receive psychiatric treatment is greater than the proportion of younger people who receive this.

3.4 The divorce rate is higher among patients with severe head injury as a result of alcoholism more than from other causes.

3.5 The CAGE alcohol-screening questionnaire is more useful in identifying established drinking alcohol problems than the AUDIT alcohol-screening questionnaire.

3.6 At post-mortem, about 30–50% of patients with acquired immunodeficiency syndrome show neuropathological changes.

3.7 Psychogenic pain rarely responds to moderate intake of alcohol.

3.8 In Wilson's disease, psychotic symptoms respond to d-penicillamine.

3.9 Energy being worse in the morning is not a useful clinical symptom to differentiate between endogenous and neurotic depression

3.10 In patients with Alzheimer's disease, phosphorylated tau and paired helical filament tau are increased about two-fold in comparison to controls.

3.11 Odds ratios will tend towards risk ratios and rate ratios as the incidence of disease falls.

3.12 The defence mechanisms in St. John's dance were denial and dissociation.

3.13 Carers of individuals with Alzheimer's disease are at high risk of developing serious immune deficiency disturbances.

3.14 More abnormalities are seen on the electroencephalogram in Alzheimer's disease than in Pick's disease.

3.15 Since the onset of civil unrest in Northern Ireland suicide rates there have increased.

3.16   Post-concussion disorder lasting more than a year is not commonly associated with litigious behaviour.

3.17   Anticipatory grief brought on by a dying loved one often softens the grief process at the time of actual death.

3.18   Aeropsia is particularly associated with cannabis abuse.

3.19   The OPCRIT computerised scoring system is used to facilitate a multi-diagnostic approach to affective disorders.

3.20   In bipolar affective disorder, manias followed by depression more commonly respond to lithium than depressions switching into mania.

3.21   In the sexual harassment of a male, a female perpetrator is slightly more common than a male perpetrator.

3.22   Among patients with schizophrenia, males are more likely to have experienced birth complications.

3.23   In Kuf's disease (cerebral ceroid lipofuscinosis), lipofuscin deposits are laid down in the basal ganglia, brainstem and cerebellum.

3.24   Emile Durkheim used the term *supra-individuality* to indicate the group as an entity more than an incidental number of members.

3.25   Large family size is associated with a decreased risk of suicide.

3.26   Increased numbers of $GABA_A$ receptors in the prefrontal cortex have been found in individuals with schizophrenia.

3.27   Hallevorden-Spatz syndrome presents usually in childhood with an extrapyramidal motor disorder and dementia.

3.28   Transvestism is more common in social class I.

3.29   In acute schizophrenia, the most frequent symptom is not persecutory delusions.

3.30   The Royal College of Psychiatrists' consensus statement regarding continuation drug therapy after a depressive episode indicates that antidepressants should be continued for at least six months after remission.

3.31   In normal pressure hydrocephalus mental changes usually appear after changes in gait and urinary incontinence.

3.32   Hypercalcaemia is not a common cause of organic catatonic disorder.

3.33   L-Tryptophan induced prolactin secretion is not reduced in panic disorder and obsessive compulsive disorder.

3.34   A family history of bipolar disorder is very strongly predictive of the prophylactic efficacy of lithium.

3.35   A one-way ANOVA with two groups is equivalent to the two-sample t test.

3.36 Payne described the cognitive defect theory, which refers to the failure of a theoretical filter that should separate background noise from useful signals.

3.37 Brown and Harris reported a significant association of childhood abuses and depression in adulthood.

3.38 The efficacy of clomipramine has been demonstrated in the pharmacological treatment of trichotillomania.

3.39 In systemic rheumatoid vasculitis involving the central nervous system (CNS), involvement of the CNS may precede joint disease.

3.40 In the absence of paternal violence, sons of alcohol-dependent men do not tend to have reduced central serotonergic turnover rates.

3.41 Life events have significant influences both on the onset and course of depression.

3.42 In the psychotherapeutic treatment of personality disorders, real motivation on the part of the patient is a requirement for treatment success.

3.43 Post-traumatic stress disorder is a recognised consequence of childbirth.

3.44 The ninth edition of the *Present State Examination* includes 299 symptom items.

3.45 Nigerians have a higher incidence of mania than depression.

3.46 With regard to neuroimaging in the elderly, late-onset depressive disorders have been distinguished from early-onset depressive disorders by the presence of hyperintensities in deep white matter on magnetic resonance imaging (MRI) T2 scanning.

3.47 Tryptophan depletion in patients with obsessive-compulsive disorder reduces their mood and exacerbates their symptoms.

3.48 White matter hyperintensities and hypointensities in the brain have been reported in late-life depression.

3.49 Usually, the brain in Creutzfeldt-Jakob disease appears normal to naked-eye inspection.

3.50 Among the elderly, the prevalence of schizophrenia decreases with age.

3.51 According to Durkheim, fatalistic suicide is the opposite of egoistic suicide.

3.52 Ninety percent of patients exhibiting obsessive slowness are male.

3.53 In progressive supranuclear palsy, neurofibrillary tangles contain ubiquitin antigens.

3.54 Sustained concentration is adversely affected by the ageing process.

3.55 The clinical features of late-onset and early-onset mania are similar.

3.56 With regard to the phobia of blood-taking and receiving injections, the response to the phobic stimulus is a bradycardia.

3.57 Mortality is higher in mania than in depression in old age.

3.58 In elderly patients, a diminished thyrotropin response to thyrotropin-releasing hormone may be used to differentiate the impaired cognitive function of pseudodementia from that of Alzheimer's disease.

3.59 Seizure threshold changes inversely with increasing age.

3.60 Tardive dyskinesia is infrequent with Crow's Type 1 schizophrenia.

3.61 Hysterical symptoms are an exception to the adage that neurotic symptoms in the elderly have the same significance in terms of diagnosis as they do in younger patients.

3.62 In the elderly, the functional psychiatric disorder most associated with the Charles-Bonnet syndrome is a severe depressive episode.

3.63 Both working memory and short-term memory decline with age.

3.64 Follow-up studies on sexual offenders show that the recidivism rate generally declines over time.

3.65 When compared to other age groups, psychiatric morbidity following bereavement is more common in old age.

3.66 Annual incidence rates for dementia are similar using ICD-10 and DSM-III-R but the individuals diagnosed may differ.

3.67 For a diagnosis of panic disorder in ICD-10, several severe attacks of autonomic anxiety should have occurred within the past two weeks.

3.68 It has been shown that there is a higher incidence of depression in married women with children than in childless married women.

3.69 According to Bergmann, the 'isolated lonely' elders have the capacity to live alone.

3.70 Cluster C personality disorders are not less prevalent in elderly populations when compared to younger populations.

3.71 One in five elderly Britons live in any type of institutional care.

3.72 The reported higher risk of suicide in individuals with low cholesterol is particularly true in males.

3.73 *Biographical death* does not refer to institutional living.

3.74 The proportion of elderly people who have alcohol dependence with poor outcome is in the region of 25%.

3.75 Clozapine use in the elderly has been associated with a decline in memory function.

3.76 There is widespread agreement that depersonalisation plays an important role in the aetiology of the Cotard Syndrome.

3.77 The risk of delirium tremens begins at 16 units of alcohol consumption per day.

3.78 The withdrawal syndrome of caffeine usually lasts about three days.

3.79 Sleep apnoea occurs in more than 25% of elderly living in institutional care.

3.80 Widely studied in Alzheimer's disease research, the β-amyloid protein (A β) is not a pathological metabolic product.

3.81 Mortality rates are lower in those who drink less than 4 units of alcohol per week.

3.82 One may diagnose a psychotic disorder due to the use of hallucinogens in the context of hallucinogen harmful use using ICD-10.

3.83 In electroencephalographic (EEG) studies, when compared to controls the sons of alcoholics show an excess of slow wave activity.

3.84 In prion diseases, the normal protein (PrP^c) and the abnormal protein (PrP^{sc}) do not differ in their amino acid sequences.

3.85 Nearly one fifth of cocaine abusers become chronic users.

3.86 The heaviest drinking in females does not tend to occur in those with unskilled manual occupations.

3.87 The prognosis for patients with Korsakoff's syndrome is better in those that have a sudden onset than those with an insidious onset.

3.88 Right-sided frontal pathology is commonly associated with 'reduplicative paramnesia'.

3.89 Repeated intentional voiding of urine alone is not sufficient to make a diagnosis of enuresis.

3.90 Cocaine is hydrolysed by pseudocholinesterase.

3.91 Dipsomania is an outmoded term and is no longer used in ICD-10.

3.92 Auditory hallucinations in alcoholic hallucinosis usually refer to the individual in the second person.

3.93 DSM-IV classifies *Reactive Attachment Disorder of Infancy or Early Childhood* into 'Inhibited' and 'Excited' subtypes.

3.94 Risperidone is useful in the treatment of visual 'flashbacks' following lysergic acid diethylamide (LSD) use.

3.95 Repeated intoxication with cocaine causes a decrease in tolerance to its use.

3.96 In Jellinek's typology of alcohol misuse, *beta alcoholism* refers to heavy drinking complicated by physical damage without physical or psychological dependence.

3.97 Dextroamphetamine does not produce ego-dystonic compulsive behaviour.

3.98 The National Comorbidity Survey found the prevalence of lifetime heroin use to be 1.5% in the United States of America.

3.99 Phenylcyclidine causes analgesia, amnesia, vertical nystagmus and depressed mood.

3.100 The visuo-spatial defects that occur in chronic alcohol dependence syndrome can be localised to the parietal lobe on the non-dominant side.

3.101 Denial is common in both manic and attention deficit hyperactive disorder (ADHD) children.

3.102 Patients on combination therapy of clonidine and 40 mg daily of methadone for opioid detoxification must not abruptly discontinue the methadone but can go through a reducing regime more quickly than if clonidine were not used.

3.103 Per capita alcohol consumption is higher among the medical profession than other professions.

3.104 Among different socio-cultural attitudes described by Pittman, the permissive societies have the lowest risk of alcoholism.

3.105 In specific reading retardation, conduct disorder is often secondary to specific reading difficulties.

3.106 While Rutter *et al.* found that various psychosocial risk factors had increased for children and adolescents since World War II, one improvement noted was that the gap between the aspirations of the young and the opportunities for achieving these had narrowed.

3.107 The Scottish Guidelines are useful for their description of the treatment of stimulant dependence with bromocriptine and anti-depressants.

3.108 It has been found that the female rate of problem drinking rises in old age.

3.109 When a child wakes up in night terror, the child can only be comforted after a while.

3.110 The prevalence of psychiatric disorder among community-living children and adolescents is in the region of 15%.

3.111 The four categories in the Adult Attachment Interview are: Dismissing, Autonomous, Unresolved/Disorganised and Resistant/Ambivalent.

3.112 Thallium poisoning may lead to the occurrence of cerebral and cerebellar calcification with chronic exposure.

3.113 Parent-adolescent alienation commonly leads to psychiatric morbidity.

3.114 On interviewing, younger children are not more inaccurate than older children in recalling information.

3.115 Obsessive symptoms in Gilles de la Tourette Syndrome have a good long-term prognosis in contrast to childhood onset obsessive-compulsive disorder.

3.116 With regards to psychiatric history taking, the process of diagnosis is nomothetic whereas the formulation is an idiographic process.

3.117 The proportion of females who become pregnant as teenagers is greater than the proportion of males who father pregnancies as teenagers.

3.118 Around 20% of children with obsessive-compulsive disorder have at least one parent with the disorder.

3.119 Boys appraise recent life events as more personally threatening than girls do.

3.120 In the pharmacotherapy of treatment resistant depression, if one opts for combining a tricyclic antidepressant (TCA) with a selective serotonin reuptake inhibitor (SSRI), one should not use citalopram since its weak cytochrome P450 inhibition means it has negligible effects in raising TCA plasma levels.

3.121 Female prisoners have a high prevalence of post-traumatic stress disorder.

3.122 The association of a psychiatric disorder with enuresis is more likely in girls.

3.123 Early aloofness is a recognised feature of autism and Asperger's syndrome.

3.124 Medroxyprogesterone acetate (Depo-Provera) has been advocated strongly for the treatment of serious hypoxyphilia.

3.125 Nearly 5% of shoplifters tend to have a diagnosis of major mood disorder.

3.126 The *Child and Adolescent Psychiatric Assessment* is a semi-structured interview for identification of psychiatric disorders in younger patients.

3.127 Heller's syndrome often presents with severe mental retardation associated with loss of bladder and bowel control in the neonatal period.

3.128 The DiGeorge syndrome and velo-cardio-facial syndrome that result from microdeletions are clinically overlapping syndromes.

3.129 In a doctor-patient relationship, privilege of the patients applies only to the legal and judicial context.

3.130 The prevalence of 'faddy eating' is higher in four year olds than in three year olds.

3.131 Hyperfrontality has been a consistent finding in magnetic resonance imaging (MRI) studies of childhood autism.

3.132 'Cocktail party' speech is a feature of Angelman's syndrome.

3.133 The incidence of infanticide in Britain is not more than two per year.

3.134 It is possible to give a dual diagnosis of autism and hyperkinetic disorder using ICD-10.

3.135 Children placed with adopted families can do well even after periods of institutionalisation up to the age of four years.

3.136 Kraepelin thought that the psychosis was independent of intellectual disability in dementia praecox arising in people with learning disability.

3.137 The risk of repeating child abduction is less common in psychotic women.

3.138 In Great Britain, among prisoners who commit suicide there is an excess of those who are serving life-sentences.

3.139 Insecure attachment occurs more frequently in severe asthmatic preschool children in comparison with healthy controls.

3.140 To make a diagnosis of *West syndrome* the following three elements should be present: infantile spasms, hypsarrhythmia on the electroencephalogram and moderate learning disability.

3.141 The re-offending rate for arson is 15%.

3.142 Around 5–8% of female children experience unequivocal sexual assault.

3.143 Babies born to teenage mothers have a high incidence of neurological deficits.

3.144 Separation from their mother in the neonatal period is regarded as a risk characteristic in an abused child.

3.145 Nearly 30% of incest perpetrators are paedophiles.

3.146 According to the Isle of Wight study, the presence of brain damage in association with epilepsy increased the risk of psychiatric illness in the individual 10-fold.

3.147 Of children and adolescents who have an episode of deliberate self-harm, roughly one-third have had a previous episode of self-harm.

3.148 Over any given year, the proportion of adolescents who have had serious suicidal ideation is in the region of 5%.

3.149 The DSM-IV diagnostic entity 'mental retardation severity unspecified' can only be used when the presumed IQ is less than 70.

3.150 Although macro-orchidism is notably associated with fragile X syndrome, only about half of individuals exhibit it after puberty.

3.151 Selective mutism has an equal sex incidence.

3.152 Structural family therapy involves the concepts of *first-order* and *second-order change*.

3.153 Aicardi syndrome is a X-linked learning disability syndrome.

3.154 Multiple incidence of learning difficulties in the same family has not been associated with social class.

3.155 The male to female gender distribution of committing officially recognised crimes is roughly 5:1.

3.156 Part of the early work in interpersonal psychotherapy for depression is trying to determine which relationships over the patient's life history have had a role in the aetiology of the depressive symptoms.

3.157 The *functional analysis* approach to the management of challenging behaviour in individuals with learning disability theoretically covers approaches such as *differential reinforcement of incompatible behaviours* and *punishment*.

3.158 Individuals with mild learning difficulties have a higher proportion of parents with low I.Q. than individuals with severe learning difficulties.

3.159 The psychiatric classification of normal homicides includes: political homicides, homicides during emotions of anger and jealousy, and homicides by people with learning disability.

3.160 In the Republic of Ireland, the decision as to whether an individual is 'unfit to plead' lies with the jury rather than with a medical assessment of the person.

3.161 In learning disabilities, destructive behaviours are the least responsive to positive behavioural interventions.

3.162 Successful surgical intervention in hydrocephalus in infants is not associated with severe mental retardation.

3.163 Trends in admission to special hospitals in Great Britain over the past ten years show an increase in the number of female offenders.

3.164 An accused who has committed a crime under a partial delusion is judged as if the facts with respect to which the delusion exists were real.

3.165 For learning disabled people *mainstreaming* is not superior over separate special education classes.

3.166 In fragile X syndrome, individuals who display mental retardation typically have between 250 and 1000 of the CAG trinucleotide repeats.

3.167 Among the learning-disabled population, court disposals to hospitals has decreased in spite of an increase in the number of arrests.

3.168 Within the prison population, serious mental illness is more common in female prisoners than male prisoners.

3.169 The prevalence of co-morbid psychiatric disorders among learning disabled persons is around 40%.

3.170 The *Autism Diagnostic Interview* is based on DSM-IV diagnostic criteria.

3.171 In neonates with Down's syndrome, muscular hypotonia is a nearly universal finding.

3.172 Under English law there are a number of restrictions regarding responsibility for criminal acts up to the age of 16 years.

3.173 Prenatal factors are responsible for 40% of severe mental retardation.

3.174 Commitment of the carers towards behavioural modification therapy in the treatment of behavioural problems in patients with learning difficulties is an important prerequisite.

3.175 In studies of re-offending in dangerous patients, shorter hospital stays and older age of offender were strongly correlated with re-offending.

3.176 *Functional communication training* is a behavioural technique used in the treatment of challenging behaviour.

3.177 Attachment theory views agoraphobia as a result of segregated emotional schemata from explicit semantic structures.

3.178 The term, *masquerade syndrome*, has been used to describe a form of hypochondriasis in which an adult uses his pre-existing chronic illness as a reason for not returning to work.

3.179 In British social service secure units, suicidal behaviours are more likely among young people with learning disability than their peers without learning disability.

3.180 Wolfensberger was a supporter of *normalisation* and *social role valorisation*.

3.181 A low dependency and high hostility attachment style is associated with a lower incidence of depression than the high dependency and high hostility attachment style.

3.182 While performing the face-hand test to elicit soft neurological signs, when stimuli are delivered simultaneously to hand and face the distal stimulus is typically extinguished.

3.183 Borderline intellectual functioning is not recognised as a category by either ICD-10 or DSM-IV.

3.184 Jung established four psychological types: sensation, thinking, feeling and intuition.

3.185 Depression is more commonly associated with losing the mother by separation before the age of six.

3.186 The most severe form of akinetic mutism results from left medial frontal lobe lesions.

3.187 Psychodynamic interpersonal therapy is a manualised therapy formerly known as the conversational model of Hobson.

3.188 In cognitive behaviour therapy, it is a recognised technique that the therapists would use examples from their own lives to help modify their patient's beliefs.

3.189 At times aversive conditioning involves both classical and operant conditioning concepts.

3.190 In bilateral posterior cerebral artery infarction, a patient cannot distinguish a car from a bus but can identify their colours.

3.191 In the practice of psychoanalytical psychotherapy with a deaf patient, insightful work requires that the patient be adept at lip-reading or the therapist is skilled in sign language.

3.192 With regard to families with a child who has a learning disability, the 'fantasy stage' of acceptance can cause families to become fixated in denial if not challenged.

3.193 Children institutionalised during their first two years are unlikely to develop normal intellectual functioning even if they are restored to their biological family.

3.194 Treatment with minor tranquillisers may reduce the suicidal risk in depressed patients.

3.195 The four dimensions of temperament in Cloninger's psycho-biological model of temperament and character are as follows: novelty seeking, harm avoidance, self-transcendence and persistence.

3.196 In cognitive behavioural therapy for body dysmorphic disorder, validation of the patient's beliefs forms an important part of therapy.

3.197 In an institutional setting, elderly people with limited personal control are better adjusted than the elderly with greater personal control.

3.198 Psychological autopsy studies indicate that in the majority of cases of suicide with alcohol dependence syndrome, co-morbid major depression was present from the early stages of alcohol use.

3.199 An example of ideational apraxia is the inability to touch parts of the face with a specified finger.

3.200 *Syllgomania* is synonymous with *Diogenes syndrome*.

Question Paper 4: Basic Sciences

4.1 Multiple bereavements significantly undermine both self-trust and other trust.

4.2 Newborn infants prefer the voice of their father to the voices of other men.

4.3 According to Kohlberg in his cognitive development theory, children develop gender identity by attending to the same sex models.

4.4 The deferred initiation paradigm correlates with Piaget's period of concrete operations.

4.5 Alicia Liberman warns that raising attachment to the status of a primary motivational system will interfere with the understanding of the complex process of development.

4.6 Piaget termed the confusion children operating on the pre-operational stage of cognitive development have between physical and moral laws as *moral realism.*

4.7 Transformational grammar allows humans to produce and understand sentences no one else has produced before.

4.8 Allochiria refers to the inability to make meaningful associations to objects that are visually present.

4.9 Homosexual pair bonds are less long lasting than heterosexual pair bonds.

4.10 The sensorimotor stage of development in Piaget's classification is not considered to be a separate developmental stage by some authors.

4.11 A child shows attachment behaviours mainly when he is returned to his attachment figure.

4.12 It has been found that firstborn children tend to be more impulsive than later children.

4.13 An 'insecure avoidant' child later developing a corresponding personality structure can be viewed as an example of healthy development based on evolutionary theory.

4.14 Infant monkeys prefer an artificial mother figure that has a rocking motion to one that is immobile.

4.15 Gender role is an individual's perception and self-awareness with respect to gender.

4.16 The Sapir-Whorf hypothesis, referring to the idea that the linguistic ability of an individual can determine his thoughts, was developed after studying Native Americans.

4.17 Self-esteem damages among employers are not uncommonly found when they lose their jobs because of economic circumstances.

4.18 Both Vygotsky and Chomsky agree that in early childhood language and thought processes develop independently.

4.19 The *generalisation gradient* describes the phenomenon that the more a stimulus is similar to the conditioned stimulus the more likely it is to produce a response and the stronger that response is likely to be.

4.20 The *supervisory attentional system* was proposed to explain the behaviour of patients with frontal lobe impairment.

4.21 An independent partner is prone to develop chronic grief when the overtly 'dependent' other partner dies.

4.22 Couples that are not satisfied with their relationship tend to be less able in understanding the non-verbal content of utterances sent by strangers than are couples that are satisfied with their relationships.

4.23 Injection of two drugs in sequence may be considered to be a Pavlovian pairing of one drug as a conditioned stimulus and the second drug as an unconditioned stimulus.

4.24 The *theta phenomenon* describes our tendency to see an instantaneous disappearance of an object and its reappearance elsewhere as movement of that object.

4.25 A situation in which a person finds himself incapable of helping an accident victim will give rise to depression.

4.26 In the Signal Detection Theory, auditory perception is considered to be mainly a function of the intensity of sound percepts, such that the function of stimulus intensity versus detection is an inverted U-shaped curve.

4.27 Premack's Principle states that a high frequency behaviour can be used to reinforce a low frequency behaviour.

4.28 According to Plutchik, the functional aspect of the primary emotion of acceptance is reproduction.

4.29 Close relationships in the workplace have the properties of childhood attachment.

4.30 Females classified as having high *androgyny* on the Bem Sex Role Inventory have been found to have a lower prevalence of psychiatric symptoms.

4.31 In focused attention, one type of information is selected for attention while the alternative information is not processed simultaneously.

4.32 With regard to Sheldon's body types, the corresponding temperament for a mesomorphic body type is somatotonic.

4.33 Main termed avoidant strategies but not the ambivalent strategies, as a 'second best strategy' to ensure parental protection.

4.34 The need for competence is considered to be lower on Maslow's Hierarchy of Needs than that for knowledge.

4.35 In operant conditioning extinction bursts are only seen in animals.

4.36 The *Barnum effect* describes how individuals accept as correct generalised and vague descriptions of themselves that have a high base-rate occurrence in the general population.

4.37 Interactive behaviours during activity-based play among 6-year-olds are more likely to be associated with their attachment characteristics to their father.

4.38 The classification of love proposed by Lee (1976) sets out six major types of relationships in which this forms of this emotion occurs, including *eros* and *mania*.

4.39 Living in a bilingual home is a cause of slower language development.

4.40 *Stimulus equivalence* refers to the situation where stimuli similar to the conditioned stimulus used in training elicit the conditioned response.

4.41 Unipolar depressed mothers tend to have more insecurely attached children in comparison to bipolar affectively ill mothers.

4.42 Schachter (1957) described that on various indices of physiological response, the sensation of pain is associated with a response similar to that produced by adrenaline.

4.43 *Proactive inhibition* suggests that new learning is likely to impair previous learning.

4.44 Allport's trait theory drew distinctions between cardinal, central and secondary traits.

4.45 At the age of ten, early insecure children tend to have more friends than early secure children.

4.46 Traditional models of the process of socialization have seen it as a mainly multidirectional process.

4.47 *Moral career* is the gradual change in perception by patients about themselves after leaving institutional care.

4.48 The Minnesota Multiphasic Personality Inventory was empirically devised to discriminate among people who had been assigned various psychiatric diagnoses.

4.49 The long lasting affect ional bonds between couples in an enduring martial relationship are similar in characteristic to long lasting kinships bonds.

4.50 In situations where men and women may choose their partners freely, women tend to choose partners who are older and more intelligent than they are.

4.51 Emile Durkheim viewed deviance as facilitating social integration.

4.52 *Motion after-effect* is thought to be important in Gestalt psychology for the production of *selective adaptation*.

4.53 The studies of Brown and Harris indicate that losses by death in childhood may be related to psychotic symptoms in depression following any kind of losses in the future.

4.54 With regard to Allport's trait theory, cardinal traits are observed in only a few people.

4.55 Patients with frontal lobe lesions may present with the following symptoms: witzelsucht, moria and pallilalia.

4.56 Anosognosia is particularly associated with right parietal lesions.

4.57 Secure individuals do not differ in their working memory processing capacity but do in their sophisticated theories of knowledge from less secure individuals.

4.58 Administration of lysergic acid diethylamide (LSD) can lead to similar increased habituation on neuropsychological testing as is seen in patients with schizophrenia, thus adding support to the dopamine hypothesis of schizophrenia.

4.59 In *connectionism* cognitive processing is viewed as occurring through the co-operation of a large number of interconnected simple processing units.

4.60 Retinal disparity is an important binocular depth cue.

4.61 Bowlby's hypothesis of multiple models is no more than a version of Freud's hypothesis of a dynamic unconsciousness.

4.62 In Marr's theory of visual perception, in which three stages are described, the final integrative stage is the *viewer-centred representation*.

4.63 The *encoding deficit theory* emphasises a storage or registration deficit in amnesia.

4.64 The anatomical correlate of auditory verbal short-term memory is the left temporo-occipital area.

4.65 According to Bowlby, sucking and clinging responses are less important attachment behaviours than the crying and following responses.

4.66 *Letter-by-letter* reading refers to a form of dyslexia in which the patient can successfully read each letter of a word but cannot tell at any stage what word these letters made up.

4.67 Prejudice often involves the use of group stereotypes and may be positive or negative.

4.68 Hegemony was a Marxist theory proposed by Antonio Gramsci.

4.69 The internal working model of attachment theory proposes that multiple internal representations are essential to effectively deal with a stressful situation.

4.70 From ethology, the generally larger size of human males in comparison to females suggests that human ancestors were polygynous.

4.71 Compared with those who are single, widowed or divorced, few married people die younger.

4.72 The Dans-Moore thesis asserts that social stratification has harmful consequences for the operation of a society.

4.73 Bynge-Hall describes a family's attempt to correct significant others' attitudes to suit the family as a 'corrective script'.

4.74 When an individual's chosen behaviour is socially undesirable, an observer tends to infer more strongly the disposition of the individual.

4.75 The role of myth in dysfunctional families can be positive in finding solutions to current problems.

4.76 Cultural lag refers to the fact that various cultural elements change at different rates.

4.77 Carl Roger's personality theory concepts include 'inborn actualising tendency', 'organismic valuing process' and 'conditional positive regard'.

4.78 In the measurement of attitudes, the usefulness of Thurstone scales as interval scales has been established.

4.79 The Buffering Hypothesis states that in the absence of high levels of stress, social supports will show no relationship with mental health.

4.80 It is the aim of socialist feminism to create a gender-free society.

4.81 It is preferable to clarify a person's response to a Rorschach card before continuing the test with the next card.

4.82 Personality traits such as tough-mindedness and impulsivity are thought to intercorrelate to produce the second-order factor of *extraversion*.

4.83 The Self Evaluation and Social Support Schedule (SESS) designed by Brown *et al.* is a self-report questionnaire.

4.84 Merton's *Strain* theory is a means of explaining deviance in society.

4.85 Frontal lobe functionally impaired patients have difficulties learning voluntarily but not when tutored.

4.86 Epley considered that interpersonal attraction was based on the individual seeking the company of another individual because he/she desired increased sexual arousal.

4.87 Latent homosexuality is defined as repressed homosexual feelings that become manifest during psychoanalytic therapy.

4.88 The sick role as described by Parsons is the normative response to disease.

4.89 Children subjected to angry mothers are commonly securely attached.

4.90 A communication with low fear content will influence a highly anxious listener more than a relaxed listener.

4.91 Durkheim described anomic suicide as resulting from the loosening of bonds between the individual and society.

4.92 When a person faces a challenge that is greater than his skills then he resorts to a 'go with flow' attitude.

4.93 The ideothetic approach to personality combines both representational and phenomenological views of personality.

4.94 According to Sternberg, *romantic love* differs from *consummate love* in being high in all three components of love: intimacy, passion and commitment.

4.95 The resilience of a family depends on its coping strategies.

4.96 The infundibulum, medulla, and cerebellum are in the posterior cranial fossa.

4.97 The pineal gland is part of the epithalamus.

4.98 The globus pallidus receives afferent input from the putamen.

4.99 The *fasiculus cuneatus* carries information regarding vibration sense.

4.100 Lesions of the left recurrent laryngeal nerve are much more common than those of the right.

4.101 The amygdala is located in the medial temporal lobe.

4.102 The dentate gyrus is part of the Papez circuit.

4.103 In the developing embryo the anterior neuropore closes on day twenty.

4.104 The three thalamic nuclei divided by the internal medullary lamina are denoted as the mediodorsal, anterior and posterior nuclei.

4.105 Pseudobulbar palsy is typically associated with a slow shuffling gait.

4.106 Decreased regional cerebral blood flow has been seen in the right parahippocampus in panic disorder on functional neuroimaging.

4.107 Functional neuroimaging of patients with schizophrenia who display Liddle's symptoms of disorganisation show decreased regional cerebral blood flow (rCBF) in both Broca's area and the right medial prefrontal cortex.

4.108 A tendency to perseveration is found with gross frontal lobe damage.

4.109 Acquired Immunodeficiency Syndrome (AIDS) related brain lymphomas are usually solitary.

4.110 Endogenous opioids derived from proenkephalin bind primarily to δ-receptors.

4.111 Electroencephalogram (EEG) activity in the newborn consists of desynchronised delta activity.

4.112 Lesions in the prefrontal cortex of the non-dominant hemisphere can cause executive aprosodia.

4.113 In Huntington's disease, the corpus striatum and the globus pallidus are markedly atrophic.

4.114 Apoptosis does not induce an inflammatory response.

4.115 Erotic ictal manifestations predominate in males.

4.116 A visual field defect of lower quadrant homonymous hemianopia occurs with a temporal lobe lesion.

4.117 The effects of morning light treatments in seasonal depression can be mimicked by morning administration of a β-adrenergic receptor agonist.

4.118 In the phosphoinositide second messenger system, both diacylglycerol and inositol trisphosphate act by activating a protein kinase.

4.119 Sodium influxes or potassium effluxes are needed for neurotransmitter release.

4.120 The calmodulins are found throughout the body and are involved with the activation of ATPase.

4.121 In patients with post-traumatic stress disorder (PTSD), low levels of plasma cortisol are significantly associated with higher numbers of lymphocyte glucocorticoid receptors.

4.122 In Alzheimer's disease, affected cholinergic neurons have increased levels of mRNA coding for nerve growth factor.

4.123 Zwitterions are amino acids that are ionised at physiological pH.

4.124 Stress causes a reduction in the synthesis of arachidonic acid.

4.125 Neuroradiological studies have shown that brain asymmetries are less striking in right-handed individuals than in left-handed individuals.

4.126 Elevated levels of cortisol, corticotropin-releasing hormone and growth hormone are found in depressive disorders.

4.127 Regarding neuropeptide transmission, neuropeptides have low receptor affinity and very little neuronal re-uptake.

4.128 In general, antidepressant drugs increase beta wave activity on the electroencephalogram.

4.129 Circulating dopamine levels can be significantly higher in head injury patients who have a Glasgow Coma Scale score of 4.

4.130 In the paraventricular nucleus, neuropeptide Y contributes to the control of corticotropin-releasing factor and thyrotropin-releasing hormone release as well as having a potent appetite-inhibitory effect.

4.131 Arachidonic acid is the precursor of prostaglandin F2α.

4.132 Chloride ions are relatively impermeable when the neuronal membrane is in its resting state.

4.133 Choline acetyltransferase is unlikely to be involved in the rate-limiting step controlling acetylcholine synthesis.

4.134 Administration over several weeks of conventional antipsychotic agents leads to a persistent depolarisation of dopaminergic neurons.

4.135 5HT$_3$ antagonists include ondansetron, ketanserin and tropisetron.

4.136 5-Hydroxytryptamine release in the nucleus accumbens decreases locomotor activity.

4.137 Nicotinic cholinergic receptors in the central nervous system contain four distinct subunits arranged as a tetramer.

4.138 In antidepressant-naïve depressed patients, cerebrospinal fluid levels of somatostatin release inhibitory factor (SRIF) are reduced.

4.139 Kline was the first to observe the antidepressant action of imipramine.

4.140 Women taking lamotrigine who wish to rely on an oral contraceptive pill should be given a preparation with at least 50 µg oestradiol.

4.141 Topiramate does not antagonise the L-AP4 and ACPD subtypes of glutamate receptors.

4.142 *d*-amphetamine and *l*-amphetamine differ in their effects on noradrenaline release.

4.143 Buspirone exerts its clinical effect through a direct action on GABA (γ-aminobutyric acid) systems.

4.144 Rapid rehydration in individuals on SSRIs may cause central pontine myelinosis.

4.145 The efficacy of propranalol in akathisia is thought to be mediated by an adrenergic β_2-receptor mechanism.

4.146 Neuroleptic malignant syndrome has been associated with pergolide therapy.

4.147 Tachyphylaxis has been shown for the sedative effects of benzodiazepines.

4.148 In acute intoxication with β-phenylisopropylamine, alkalinisation of the urine increases excretion.

4.149 Concurrent use of erythromycin with alprazolam may increase the level of alprazolam by two-fold.

4.150 Fluphenazine decanoate exhibits a similar time to steady state as does haloperidol decanoate.

4.151 Noticeable adverse effects of paroxetine include a withdrawal syndrome and lowering of the seizure threshold.

4.152 Skin rashes due to drug treatment are an example of a Type I hypersensitivity reaction.

4.153 Masochism is associated with over-compliance to prescribed treatment.

4.154 Since it undergoes moderate first-pass metabolism, only about a quarter of the amount of buspirone taken orally reaches the systemic circulation.

4.155 Dose related adverse effects of carbamazepine include dizziness, diplopia and ataxia.

4.156 Pharmacokinetic studies of donepezil hydrochloride show that caution should be exercised when it is used along with carbamazepine because of inhibition of CYP2D6 and CYP3A4 enzymes.

4.157 Ampakines are not associated with changes in cognitive performances.

4.158 Although they all act by allosterically modulating the GABA$_A$ (γ-aminobutyric acid) receptor, there are separate receptor binding sites for benzodiazepines, barbiturates and alcohol.

4.159 Factors that increase the volume of drug distribution include high lipid solubility, a higher proportion of adipose tissue and younger age.

4.160 It has been found that carbamazepine may increase lithium-induced polyuria.

4.161 Ketamine at high doses does not cause narcosis.

4.162 In the treatment of obsessive-compulsive disorder with selective serotonin reuptake inhibitors, after three months the average patient response is about a one-third reduction in symptoms.

4.163 Issues of reverse causality are best addressed by using case control studies.

4.164 The '5% trimmed mean' is the data remaining after excluding the highest and lowest 5% of values.

4.165 Non-clinicians can administer Schedule for Affective Disorders and Schizophrenia.

4.166 A diagnostic test that has a high specificity tends to rule out diagnoses.

4.167 While the General Health Questionnaire is used frequently in large-scale surveys, it has high rates of false positives among the physically ill.

4.168 A type I, or alpha, error is less common than a type II, or beta error.

4.169 A high score in the 60 items General Health Questionnaire may indicate a specific non-psychotic diagnosis.

4.170 The mode is usually more appropriate for data of a study that are of nominal scale in nature than is the median.

4.171 The arcsine transformation is a mathematical transformation that is appropriate for reciprocals.

4.172 With regard to population screening, the preferred study design is a cohort study.

4.173 Properly consented unnecessary researches are not unethical.

4.174 When comparing means of observations in a 2 × 2 contingency table, where the total of one of the cells is less than 10, one should use Yeats' correction to the χ^2 test.

4.175 A Galbraith Plot is a plot of the standard normal deviate against the reciprocal of the standard error.

4.176 A *sensitivity analysis* of a systematic review involves adjusting the criteria used by the reviewer to determine whether the key findings remain constant.

4.177 The standard error of the mean is a good index of variability in data from research studies.

4.178 The ranking of doctors, such as senior house officer or specialist registrar, is an example of an ordinal scale.

4.179 Pleiotropy refers to the situation whereby the same gene has two or more apparently different effects.

4.180 *Annealing* refers to the process that causes duplex deoxyribonucleic acid (DNA) to unwind into single strands.

4.181 Epistasis can refer to the phenotypic expression of a gene inter-action with another gene on a different chromosome.

4.182 Prader-Willi syndrome is associated with uniparental disomy of chromosome 15 where both chromosomes come from the mother.

4.183 Recombination fractions can vary from 0 to 1.0.

4.184 A *neutral gene* is a gene that has undergone mutation to one that has no gene product.

4.185 Cloninger type II alcoholism is associated with either of the biological parents having alcohol dependency.

4.186 Because of their relative insensitivity, association studies are less suitable for the study of the genetic components of pathogenesis of most psychiatric disorders than are linkage studies.

4.187 Penetrance is the probability of manifesting a trait given a certain phenotype.

4.188 Cytoplasmic inheritance refers to genetic material involved in energy-yielding reactions.

4.189 Deoxyribonucleic acid (DNA) and protein stains can identify chromosomal inversions.

4.190 In genetic linkage analysis, most restriction fragment length polymorphisms (RFLPs) that arise from single base substitutions and variable number of tandem repeats (VNTRs) are biallelic.

4.191 Mitochondrial deoxyribonucleic acid (DNA) inheritance is solely paternal.

4.192 There is a higher risk of abortion with chorionic villus biopsy than with amniocentesis.

4.193 Kendler proposes that hereditary factors influence the behavioural reaction to non-significant life events.

4.194 In quantitative genetics, the *Hardy-Weinberg equilibrium* assumes that there is no mutation in the population.

4.195 In epidemiology, Poisson distribution statistics are used to manipulate incidence rates.

4.196 Non-randomised evidence is of no value when there exists a good understanding of the confounding variables that affect prognosis.

4.197 Computer interview is a less stigmatising and a less expensive method than a personal interview.

4.198 For the population attributable fraction (PAF) to be low a disease should have a small relative risk and there should be a common exposure.

4.199 *Cost-effectiveness analysis* is used when the effect of the intervention on health analysis has two or more important dimensions.

4.200 The lifetime prevalence of agoraphobia, as determined by the Epidemiological Catchment Area Study, is approximately 5%.

Question Paper 5: Basic Sciences

5.1 A mother's multiple facets of roles as a playmate, as a caregiver and as a teacher with her infant are commonly responsible for attachment having evolved.

5.2 In Piaget's preoperational stage, children may be able to centre attention on more than one aspect of the task at a time.

5.3 Regarding attachment, separation of an infant from its caregiver prior to six months or after three years of age has little effect.

5.4 Studies have shown that twins develop language skills at a faster rate than singletons.

5.5 In a strange situation the majority of one-year-old children do not show good sociable behaviour upon encountering an adult stranger when the mother is present.

5.6 The development of *semiotic function* marks the onset of the preoperational period of cognitive development according to Piaget.

5.7 Finalism is a thought process exhibited during the concrete operational stage.

5.8 Providing premature babies with human breast milk through a nasogastric tube improves their cognitive development at a later age.

5.9 Long lasting childhood friendship often needs congeniality of interests but is less dependent on proximity keeping.

5.10 About half of infants will be able to sit without support at 4½ months of age.

5.11 According to the Sapir-Whorf hypothesis, language determines our available concepts and these concepts limit our scope for thought.

5.12 Donaldson describes *embedded thinking* as a process of cognitive development.

5.13 There is strong evidence that the bonds of adult attachment are similar to the development of childhood attachment bonds.

5.14 The effects of maternal deprivation include enuresis, poor growth and aggression.

5.15 The Mannheim Interview is an instrument that measures the level of gender stereotyping attitudes that an individual holds.

5.16 Children younger than age seven can be taught that something specific is dangerous but they are unable to generalise from it.

5.17 Insecure-ambivalent (C-dyad) children more often initiate interaction with their parents with toy representations and loved vocalizations.

5.18 In psychological theories of attention, the *Stroop effect* refers to a process whereby processing is impaired rather than facilitated.

5.19 Institutional neurosis includes apathy, institutional perspective, withdrawal and low self-esteem.

5.20 The *cocktail party effect* is observed more commonly in younger subjects.

5.21 The concept that only sensitive responsive mothering will produce a socially competent individual is not compatible with evolutionary theory.

5.22 Humans of any age show a differing response from animals to fixed-interval schedules in which a reward comes from pressing a particular lever.

5.23 In *Social Labelling Theory* it is argued that it is the nature of the response to the action that constitutes deviance.

5.24 The Ravens Progressive Matrices Test is regarded as a culture-fair intelligence test.

5.25 According to Gardiner, the inhibitory effect on memorisation that proactive inhibition has does not have the most effect at encoding.

5.26 Lidz proposed the concept of abnormal family communications in patients with schizophrenia.

5.27 In a group play involving six-year-olds, former maternal sensitivity was found to be lower for the group of passively compliant children than for a group of engaged uncooperative children.

5.28 The stress-coping paradigm was developed by Seyle.

5.29 The emotional experience due to attachment difficulties during the first year of life cannot be easily compensated by later cognitive skills.

5.30 Two-weeks-old infants show no difference in their reactions to two objects of different sizes that approach to different proximities towards their face such that the infant's retinal image of both is of the same size.

5.31 Life events are significant in causing relapse in schizophrenia but not its onset.

5.32 The *ERG* theory condenses Maslow's hierarchy to three levels of need.

5.33 According to Parker, a caring and overprotective parental style predisposes to minor depressive disorder.

5.34 Rats that are given electrical shocks in the first five days after birth display more pronounced anxiety reactions as adults than those who have not received such electrical shocks.

5.35 Parsons defined abnormal illness behaviour as the individual having a 'persistence of a maladaptive mode of experiencing, perceiving, evaluating and responding' with regards to his health status.

5.36 Constancy can be found in brightness perception.

5.37 Illness can permanently change an insecure internal working model into a secure one.

5.38 When children are asked to state which men they like and dislike from a series of photographs, they tend to prefer those they think are from their own country and this trend is more marked in the older children.

5.39 Osgood's *Congruity Theory* differs from Festinger's *Dissonance Theory* in that Festinger deals with attitudes to behaviour rather than attitudes regarding other attitudes.

5.40 Background conditioning is widely used in advertising.

5.41 A person saying 'I can be successful' is using metacognitive knowledge.

5.42 A pan-cultural distribution of a characteristic implies genetic transmission of the characteristic.

5.43 Marcia's *identity diffusion* is analogous to *identity confusion* in Erikson's staging.

5.44 The *Thematic Apperception Test* is used to study an individual's hierarchy of needs.

5.45 Successful resolution of mourning the loss of a family member depends mainly on the feelings of responsibility in caring for others in the family rather than a sense of family solidarity.

5.46 In contrast to explicit memory, the components of implicit memory are present from birth.

5.47 Non-verbal short-term memory may be correlated with the non-dominant temporal lobes.

5.48 Being part of a mixed sex group is a factor known to increase conformity.

5.49 Attachment theory is too narrow a concept to be compatible with the General System Theory.

5.50 Metacognitive processes develop around the age of eight in the child.

5.51 Visual illusions can be explained by assuming that the processes used to produce size constancy with three-dimensional objects are applied to two-dimensional drawings.

5.52 Illsky found that women who were on average taller than other members of their class of origin were more likely to marry into a higher social class.

5.53 Main and Solomon have identified a distinct fourth attachment behaviour pattern – the disorganised behaviour pattern.

5.54 Damage to the angular gyrus produces an inability to write but conserves the ability to read

5.55 Dominant frontal lobe lesions may result in aprosody.

5.56 Greenwood listed a broad community sanction among the qualities required by an occupation if it is to be regarded as a profession.

5.57 A person's belief about 'locus of control' is stereotypic and it is unlikely to vary with specific situations.

5.58 The *Halstead-Reitan Neuropsychological Battery* consists of eleven components including the *Trail Making Test* and the *Minnesota Multiphasic Personality Inventory.*

5.59 The normal score for the reverse digit span in adults is two digits less than the normal score for the forward digit span when testing attention.

5.60 Frontal lobe lesions may cause motor Jacksonian fits.

5.61 Roger's *client centred therapy* used a phenomenological approach in its development and thus its theory regarding personality is considered an example of a nomethetic theory of personality.

5.62 The *National Adult Reading Test* gives a reasonable estimation of premorbid intellectual functioning in individuals with IQs greater than 80.

5.63 The *Thematic Apperception Test* consists of ten cards that depict a variety of ambiguous scenes.

5.64 In the Papez circuit, sensory information is transmitted from the thalamus to the hypothalamus.

5.65 The *NEO inventories* are not a neuropsychiatric test battery.

5.66 Weber disagreed with Marx's view of religion's effects on individuals in society, arguing that its main purpose is to give meaning to the individual's existence.

5.67 Increased cognitive dissonance occurs when there is increased pressure to comply and there is an awareness of personal responsibility for any consequences.

5.68 A *type 3 family* refers to a married couple with dependent children.

5.69 Karl Heider's work on emotional experiences considered both psychological and physiological aspects of emotions.

5.70 R. D. Laing considered that therapy for individuals with schizophrenia constituted a means of social control.

5.71 Antecedent conditions for *groupthink* include high stress, a directive leader and a cohesive group.

5.72 Switzerland represents an example of a pluralist society.

5.73 During the psychiatric interview having knowledge of anthropology significantly helps in establishing rapport.

5.74 In sociological terms, the following were deviants: Adolf Hitler, Joseph Stalin and St. Francis of Assisi.

5.75 Cognitive consistency, which is important in one's attitude to oneself, cannot be considered as a basic need.

5.76 The twentieth century has seen a move from private patriarchy to public patriarchy in Western Society

5.77 In common chimpanzees the core group mainly consists of female members who are unrelated migrants.

5.78 The *genome-lag hypothesis* draws on the concept of *expatiation*.

5.79 Functions of attitudes include the knowledge function, instrumental function and the value expressive function.

5.80 In the study of a society, what distinguishes *reciprocal altruism* from *joint cooperation* is the motivation of the individuals involved.

5.81 Psychiatrists' attempts to rehabilitate patients to medical and psychological equilibrium is unrelated to the evolutionary process.

5.82 According to evolutionary biology, depressed individuals who show social withdrawal typically set aside most of their strategies for behaviour for the duration of the disorder only, resuming these after recovery.

5.83 According to Plutchik, the primary emotions of surprise and sadness give the secondary emotion of disappointment.

5.84 The common chimpanzee (*Pan troglodytes*) is the only primate other than humans that engages in sexual intercourse for reasons other than reproduction.

5.85 The meaning of 'love' does not load with the same component throughout the world.

5.86   Evolutionary theory holds that human behaviour is best understood in terms of attempting to achieve long-term goals, particularly reproduction.

5.87   Hans Seyle states in his *General Adaption Syndrome*, that the non-specific physiological reaction to stress consists of an alarm reaction, resistance and exhaustion stages.

5.88   From an evolutionary viewpoint, the ultimate causation view of depression is not invalidated by the fact that most individuals with depression can recover on their own.

5.89   Balinese culture, by actively encouraging the bereaved to be cheerful rather than sad, has disproved the universality of grief.

5.90   The term *cultural relativism* is used to describe the difficulty that arises when a Western psychiatric diagnostic category is improperly used in a culture in which the category has no relevance.

5.91   'Fixed action pattern' is a fixed pattern of behaviour that does not depend on learning.

5.92   The anthropological term of *emic* is used in cultural psychiatry to denote the use of categories that have useful meaning to the specific culture to which they are applied.

5.93   According to neurodevelopmental theories of schizophrenia, islands of neuronal clusters occur in the superficial cortical layers of the entorhinal cortex.

5.94   The Papez circuit links the limbic system and the neocortex via the cingulate gyrus.

5.95   The majority of the nerve fibres in the crus cerebri are cortico-spinal fibres.

5.96   Axodendritic synapses are usually excitatory in their effect whereas most axosomatic synapses are inhibitory.

5.97   In the rodent's striatum dopaminergic receptors are discontinuously distributed.

5.98   The supralemniscal nucleus contains mainly serotonergic neurons.

5.99   The diencephalon consists of the hypothalamus, thalamus, hippocampus and epithalamus.

5.100 Herniation of the uncus of the temporal lobe causes a third nerve palsy.

5.101 Superior extension of a pituitary tumour causes visual symptoms.

5.102 The location of the insula is at the base of the lateral sulcus.

5.103 In the pathology of idiopathic Parkinson's disease, Lewy bodies are particularly found in the locus coeruleus and the dorsal motor nucleus of the vagus.

5.104 The *Foster Kennedy syndrome* refers to optic atrophy on the side of a frontal lobe space occupying lesion and papilloedema on the opposite side.

5.105 The neuropathological changes in fatal cases of anoxia resemble those seen after hypoglycaemia.

5.106 Astrocytes typically respond to a cerebral insult by increasing in absolute number of cells, although the total astrocytic cell volume decreases as a result of their reactive reduction in size.

5.107 The dementia that may develop during the course of Binswanger's disease typically involves a slow progression involving 'step-like' changes.

5.108 'Kindling' is a property unique to the hippocampal formation and amygdala.

5.109 Chronic arsenic poisoning does not cause significant difficulties with memory.

5.110 About 1 in 25 normal subjects show a blunted thyrotropin response to thyrotropin releasing factor administration.

5.111 The *expectancy wave* is an event-related slow potential that is attenuated by lack of stimulation.

5.112 The Kluver Bucy syndrome involves bilateral damage to the anterior portion of the temporal lobes.

5.113 Vacuolar myelin swelling of the brain in patients with the human immunodeficiency virus (HIV) is a late development.

5.114 Stimulation of the lateral zone of the hypothalamus causes a reduction in food intake.

5.115 Sleep spindles may occur during sleep stages II, III and IV.

5.116 Rapid Eye Movement sleep is associated with decreased protein synthesis in the rat brain.

5.117 Learned motor behaviours are invariably mediated by localised brain processes.

5.118 Renshaw cells are inhibitory interneurones present in the spinal cord posterior horn.

5.119 When hormones bind to receptors that are linked to G proteins, the effect of the stimulation of the receptor is to activate adenyl cyclase.

5.120 The Monro-Kellie hypothesis refers to the fact that the amount of blood in the brain is more or less constant.

5.121 An exaggerated cortisol response to a stressor can be seen if it was preceded by the exposure of the stressor by at least two days.

5.122 γ-Aminobutyric acid (GABA) acts to diminish the stimulatory action of noradrenaline on growth hormone releasing hormone release.

5.123 Aldehyde dehydrogenase is involved in the intermediate step in both catabolic pathways for the degradation of dopamine.

5.124 During the development of the central nervous system in the foetus, the rhombencephalon differentiates into the mesencephalon and the myelencephalon.

5.125 In patients with normal-pressure hydrocephalus in whom shunting has been successful, positron-emission tomography (PET) studies have shown temporal-parietal changes.

5.126 Insulin-like growth factor I has roughly two-thirds homology with insulin and acts on the hypothalamopituitary (HPA) axis to inhibit growth hormone production.

5.127 Choline acetyltransferase (CHAT) is the rate-limiting step in the production of acetylcholine from choline and acetyl CoA.

5.128 Patients with chronic fatigue syndrome have been found to have higher plasma prolactin concentrations in response to acute administration of buspirone compared to controls.

5.129 $GABA_B$ receptor potentials are not faster in onset but are longer in duration than those mediated by $GABA_A$.

5.130 The following serotoninergic receptors are linked to the phosphatidylinositol system: $5HT_{1A}$, $5HT_{2A}$, $5HT_{2B}$ and $5HT_{2C}$.

5.131 In the central nervous system, the highest concentrations of cholecystokinin are found in the cerebellum.

5.132 The cell bodies of the 'intermediate length' dopaminergic projections lie in the mesencephalon.

5.133 Transcranial magnetic stimulation (TMS) does not demonstrate a true causal connection between local stimulation and functional response.

5.134 Cerebrospinal fluid concentrations of corticotropin-releasing factor (CRF) correlate with the severity of depression in patients with anorexia nervosa.

5.135 Catecholamine synthesis can be inhibited by competitive inhibition at the pteridine-binding site.

5.136 There is no consistent evidence that glucocorticoid concentrations exhibit a circadian pattern.

5.137 *N*-Methyl-D-aspartate (NMDA) receptors subtypes NMDA-R1 and NMDA-R2 are blocked by magnesium ions.

5.138 Although temazepam has a roughly similar onset of action time to zopiclone, it has a longer duration of action.

5.139 Risperidone, in contrast to olanzapine, causes both neutropenia and agranulocytosis.

5.140 Fenfluramine is a member of the serotonergic anorectic class of drugs.

5.141 Phenytoin is more commonly associated with gaze-evoked nystagmus than pendular nystagmus.

5.142 Among the newer pharmacotherapies for bipolar affective disorder, lamotrigine is the only agent that has weight loss as a side-effect.

5.143 Facial oedema and paralytic ileus are adverse effects associated with the use of tricyclic antidepressants.

5.144 With regard to alcohol detoxification, parenteral B complex vitamins must be administered before glucose in all patients who present with an altered mental status.

5.145 Phenelzine efficacy in obsessive-compulsive disorder may be limited to patients with violent obsessive thoughts.

5.146 The time of greatest risk of teratogenic effect from drug treatment in pregnancy is the first three weeks after conception.

5.147 Marked sialorrhoea occurs in 10% of patients on clozapine.

5.148 With regard to phenothiazines, the formation of sulfoxides is an important metabolic pathway.

5.149 Temazepam is the most common benzodiazepine preferred for intravenous abuse by opioid intravenous abusers.

5.150 Roughly two-thirds of rivastigmine undergoes glucuronidation by the liver in its metabolism.

5.151 *First order kinetics* is defined as a process whereby the rate of absorption or elimination of a drug depends on the amount remaining.

5.152 Ethanol increases plasma levels of phenytoin and the barbiturates through competitive action at enzyme sites.

5.153 Levonantradol has significant antiemetic and sedative effects.

5.154 The fall in plasma tricyclic antidepressant levels as a result of concomitant smoking is generally of little clinical importance.

5.155 Phase II hepatic biotransformation involves non-synthetic reactions.

5.156 The excretion of venlafaxine is almost exclusively renal.

5.157 Compounds that inhibit protein synthesis have negative effects on long-term potentiation (LTP) and long-term maintenance of memory process.

5.158 Benzodiazepine therapy has been associated with an increased risk of hip fracture, not just anecdotally, but from research.

5.159 Late adverse effects of lithium include polyuria, oedema, anorexia and ataxia.

5.160 The concentration of lithium in bone is two to four times higher than in extracellular fluid.

5.161 Inherited cognitive abnormalities are important trait markers to be considered in genetic studies.

5.162 If the inheritance pattern of a familial disorder does not show the typical Mendelian pattern of inheritance of either one-in-four or one-in-two offspring being affected, then one may reasonably reject the idea of the disorder having a single major locus form of transmission.

5.163 The process of deoxyribonucleic acid (DNA) replication is described as semi-continuous.

5.164 The Hardy-Weinberg principle holds only under stable population conditions.

5.165 Mutations in non-coding regions do not show phenotypic effects.

5.166 An example of genomic imprinting is seen in Huntington's disease.

5.167 Probandwise concordance refers to the situation where the number of affected twins is divided by the total number of co-twins.

5.168 *Incomplete ascertainment* is a term used in restriction fragment length polymorphism (RFLP).

5.169 Direct sequencing of the gene is the most preferred technique to identify gene mutations.

5.170 Despite numerous genetic marker studies investigating the association between HLA and schizophrenia, there have not been any findings that have been replicated.

5.171 The occurrence of microdeletions at chromosome 22q11 has been associated with the risk of developing schizophrenia.

5.172 Non-transmitted genetic effects include imprinting and variation in methylation.

5.173 Severe nutritional deficiencies in the first trimester of pregnancy are associated with increased incidence of schizophrenia in the female offspring.

5.174 The human genome is thought to contain between 150,000 and 200,000 genes.

5.175 Individuals with autosomal recessive disorders display a pattern of vertical transmission.

5.176 A LOD score of 3 is taken as statistical inference of linkage.

5.177 The specificity of an instrument is the probability of diagnosing a disease when present.

5.178 The Epidemiologic Catchment Area (ECA) Program was a multi-centre epidemiological study designed to assess the prevalence of psychiatric disorders in adult community dwellers only.

5.179 The *Composite International Diagnostic Interview* is a combination of the *Diagnostic Interview Schedule* and the *Present State Examination*.

5.180 'Case finding' refers to a procedure in which a test is applied to apparently healthy volunteers to identify those with a high risk of developing an otherwise unrecognised disease.

5.181 A *power calculation* in a research study depends on deciding before-hand what would comprise a statistically significant difference in effect.

5.182 In the screening of a given population for psychiatric illness, the Present State Examination (Wing *et al.* 1974) has relatively good reliability in diagnosing schizophrenia and alcoholism, but relatively poor reliability in diagnosing personality disorders and organic conditions.

5.183 In studying epidemiology the number of cases (the floating numerator) is useful if related to the population at risk.

5.184 A cost utility analysis is employed when the effect of the intervention can be expressed in terms of one main variable.

5.185 If the 99% confidence interval does not include the value zero and if the true mean difference were zero then the hypothesis would be rejected at the 1% level.

5.186 In epidemiology, the terms *inception* and *incidence* may be used synonymously.

5.187 Inter-rater reliability Cronbach alpha values of 0.70–0.80 are required for individual screening.

5.188 A correct definition of a 95% confidence interval is that 95% of such intervals will contain the true population values.

5.189 Standardisation to a *z* score makes different quantities commen-surable.

5.190 The prevalence of a given disease is related to its incidence by the product of the latter with the chronicity of the disease.

5.191 Cost consequence analysis presents the results of the economic analysis in a form where different outcomes are expressed in their natural units.

5.192 *N-of-1* refer to trials where the patients are allocated to groups on the basis of their previous treatments.

5.193 Complementary probability is the probability of a particular outcome believed to occur more than once.

5.194 In a diagnostic test, the proportion of all tests that have been given the correct result is termed the *positive predictive value.*

5.195 In assessing test-retest reliability the product moment correlation (r) gives a higher level of agreement than the kappa statistic (κ).

5.196 The important difference between epidemiological surveys and screening is that in the former no benefit to health is implied

5.197 McNemar's test is used when the data is qualitative.

5.198 The number needed to treat (NNT) equals the reciprocal of the control event rate (CER) minus the experiment event rate (EER).

5.199 The correlation of inter-rater reliability using the Camberwell Assessment of Needs for the Elderly has been shown to be 0.7.

5.200 The pre-test probability refers to the proportion of people with the target disorder in the population at risk at a specific time or time interval.

Question Paper 6: Basic Sciences

6.1　Insecurely attached A-dyad children are more likely to initiate interaction with their parent with soft vocalizations.

6.2　Newborn infants will not prefer to look at a plain disk that does not have fine print on it over one that does.

6.3　In language development a morpheme is the essential unit of sound.

6.4　Antenatal exposure to aspirin has been found to be linked to lower IQ.

6.5　Unlike securely attached children, the majority of six-year-old insecurely attached children informed an interviewer that a child experiencing separation would feel anxious, lonely and sad.

6.6　Cognitive therapy requires that the person being treated has progressed to Piaget's formal operations stage of cognitive development.

6.7　Infants at six months have usually accomplished monotropic attachment.

6.8　With regard to phonological processes, in *fronting*, consonants that are pronounced at the back of the vocal tract are substituted for those pronounced at the front of the vocal tract.

6.9　Intense affect in response to stress is the characteristic finding in insecure mothers and depressed mothers in secure attachment relationships.

6.10　A child who has been reared by two lesbian parents has an increased risk of exhibiting emotional and behavioural problems.

6.11　A child of age 7–8 will typically realise that when a lump of clay is transformed from one shape into another its weight will be conserved.

6.12　Bottom-up processing creates expectancy and sets up what is known as 'perceptual set'.

6.13　The majority of four-year-old children can comprehend that a person can have both positive and negative emotions.

6.14　In individuals who have suffered child sexual abuse there is a higher incidence of homosexuality.

6.15 The following disorders are more likely to be diagnosed in those in lower social classes: schizophrenia, personality disorder and depressive episodes in women.

6.16 G. Stanley Hall was the founder of Functionalism.

6.17 Regarding severe anxiety occurring after bereavement, there is a more significant association with life events after bereavement contributing to the anxiety, than with parental influences during development that promote fear.

6.18 It is thought that the administration of chlorpromazine after diazepam leading to a reduced relaxant activity of diazepam results from conditioning and not just pharmacological interaction.

6.19 In escape conditioning the response prevents an aversive event occurring.

6.20 Kubler-Ross described a series of stages in the process of mourning.

6.21 In the real sense, an attachment is not an affect ional bond.

6.22 An attitude that one holds that helps one to make sense of one's environment is said to serve an *instrumental* function.

6.23 Adorno's *authoritarian personality theory* is a psychodynamic theory regarding authoritarian upbringing.

6.24 In an emotional hierarchy, categories that vary by culture are at the basic level.

6.25 According to Bowlby, multiple models of internal representation related to attachment events are completely unconscious.

6.26 In interpersonal attraction, similar scores on the personality trait of Eysenck's *psychoticism* tend to correlate.

6.27 Punishment and negative reinforcement are both examples of aversive conditioning.

6.28 According to Cohen and Lazarus, inhibition of action is one of the five main categories of coping strategies.

6.29 Recent research has supported the attachment theorists' explanation of mental suffering as the early defensive exclusion of a given idea.

6.30 Most children do not develop similar patterns of attachment behaviour when their father leaves the room in the *strange situation* as when their mother leaves.

6.31 Seligman, in his model of depression, describes the subject who is exposed to conditions in which responding has no effect on whether reinforcement occurs subsequently.

6.32 The visuospatial scratch pad is one of the components of short-term memory.

6.33 Robertson's film *A Two Years Old Goes to Hospital* explained the parental factors involved in the battered child syndrome.

6.34 According to the *facial feedback hypothesis* it is from one's own facial expression that one experiences a stronger emotional response rather than others' facial expressions.

6.35 Lazarus in the Systems Principle contends that individual emotions can be only be understood in reference to the particular patterns of appraisal.

6.36 Reintegration is a type of remembering involved in the passing on of information from one person to another.

6.37 The strange situation model is unsuitable to study attachment behaviours in different cultures.

6.38 Both rats and chimpanzees, once they have solved an experimental problem, continue to make irrelevant moves on subsequent attempts for a period of time afterwards.

6.39 When making causal attributions about an individual based on his actions, people tend to overuse consensus information.

6.40 The distinction between discreditable and discrediting stigma is that the former is associated with negative discrimination only in certain situations while the latter leads to disadvantage for the sufferer in all situations.

6.41 Representational approaches of personality are always non-deterministic.

6.42 An individual with an 'authoritarian personality' is more likely to join a fascist group.

6.43 Goldberg and Huxley's filters to psychiatric care depend on social factors, service organisation and aspects of the disorder itself.

6.44 Paralinguistic features in communication include posture, eye contact and touch.

6.45 Erikson's life stages can be measured by the *Inventory of Social Balance* personality rating scale.

6.46 Central pathways involving the presentation of cues can modify attitudes.

6.47 On neuropsychological testing, patients with schizophrenia do not show reduced reaction times when tested with varying stimuli in differing modalities in comparison to normal controls.

6.48 In organic disorders elation is not uncommonly associated with flight of ideas.

6.49 Psychological tests generally provide suitable measures of brain damage.

6.50 In the 'dual-route' model of reading, non-words may be read by processing through the non-lexical route.

6.51 Fluent dysphasia involves damage posterior to the Sylvian fissure.

6.52 Brain impaired individuals invariably present with difficulties in intellectual functioning and flexibility.

6.53 Patients with 'anterior alexia' may be able to read syntactically important words but they may not be able to read nouns and verbs.

6.54 The improved recovery that occurs after a number of smaller insults to the brain over a longer period of time than after a single larger insult, even if the total damaged areas are similar in both cases, has been referred to as the *serial-lesion effect.*

6.55 Peripheral dyslexias include neglect dyslexia, visual dyslexia, attentional dyslexia and letter-by-letter reading.

6.56 Posterior temporal lobectomy causes the 'cocktail party effect'.

6.57 Constructional apraxia is not uncommonly exhibited clinically.

6.58 Childhood amnesia may be due to the hippocampus being immature.

6.59 In long-term potentiation, the binding of glutamate to N-methyl-D-aspartate (NMDA) receptors is sufficient to allow Na^+ and Ca^{2+} ions to enter the neuron.

6.60 Offensive and unpleasant olfactory hallucinations are common in antero-inferior temporal lobe lesions.

6.61 Right temporal lobe lesions cause ear loss for tonal sequences and efficiency for digits.

6.62 Perceptual defence and perceptual sensitisation differ only in the time taken to identify a word.

6.63 The occurrence in a patient of great difficulty in copying writing but normal spelling ability locates a lesion to the dominant parietal lobe.

6.64 Right parietal lobe damaged individuals' drawings will be characteristically fragmented, energetic and have faulty orientation.

6.65 Modified leucotomy commonly produces dissociation between verbalisation and action.

6.66 Patients with colour agnosia can distinguish between colours well.

6.67 In the *Rey-Osterrieth Complex Figure Test,* abnormalities are seen in reproducing the figure in patients with lesions in: the right hemisphere, large areas of the left hemisphere, the frontal lobes and the right temporal lobe areas.

6.68 Pseudohomophones are words that conform to the rules of English but have no meaning.

6.69 Dismissing parents of avoidant infants are unlikely to be not succinct whereas preoccupied parents of ambivalent infants are less likely to be succinct.

6.70 The term *institutional neurosis* is associated with Goffman (1961).

6.71 The *F scale* is a personality questionnaire that tests tendencies towards fascism.

6.72 Marx considered that the normal state of affairs in a society is a stable period of stagnation under a capitalist regime, unless a charismatic leader emerges to lead the revolution.

6.73 The conflict of an avoidant infant is whether to withdraw or approach its rejecting mother.

6.74 The positivist framework of understanding organisational structure as proposed by workers such as Perrow is considered to be particularly suitable in understanding the working of the psychiatric multidisciplinary team.

6.75 Chomsky thought that language develops independently of other non-linguistic cognitive processes.

6.76 The situation wherein young psychotherapists use their 'feeling thought' as part of their assessment is not compatible with the anthropological approach.

6.77 Attachment theorists believe that in agoraphobia there is significant indirect evidence of emotional dysregulation during the Freudian pre-oedipal stage.

6.78 Weber considered that the best structure for a hospital in contemporary society is that of a rational/legal bureaucratic one.

6.79 The short-term memory digit span of seven plus or minus two is fixed.

6.80 Visual short-term memory is not stored in the right hemisphere.

6.81 The amount of time mothers have been separated from their newborn babies significantly predicts the differences in maternal bonding.

6.82 Merton described four types of deviant outcome to states of anomie in societies: innovation, ritualism, retreatism and rebellion.

6.83 Nativists' theories of language acquisition can be attributed to Chomsky, Greenberg and Skinner.

6.84 Single birth and nursing at least four times an hour are examples of the 'cataroline' mother-infant complex characteristics.

6.85 An understanding of sociopathy based on evolutionary adaptation can improve the rehabilitation of this behaviour.

6.86 Emile Durkheim considered that suicide acted as an impediment to social integration.

6.87 The Rorschach inkblot test can be scored and interpreted using the Exner Comprehensive System.

6.88 Paul MacLean showed that higher primates place emphasis on mother-infant bonding rather than juvenile play.

6.89 *Environment of evolutionary adaptedness* (EEA) refers to the gradual transition of a multi-aged playgroup.

6.90 The solidarity of an ethnic group tends to be strengthened by endogamy.

6.91 Clonidine induced hypoactivity is a suitable animal model to study antidepressants' efficacy.

6.92 Humans avoiding incest and thereby inbreeding by socio-cultural choice is an example of defying the evolutionary mechanism.

6.93 Absence of words to express depressive feeling in Indian culture does not mean that they do not know about how it would feel to be depressed.

6.94 *Homo sapiens* is the only species of primates that exhibits homosexual sexual intercourse.

6.95 The reticular formation is continuous with the lateral part of the hypothalamus and is involved in the righting reflexes.

6.96 Large dorsolateral frontal lobe lesions are associated with hyperkinesia, increased instinctual drives and childish humour.

6.97 The lateral ventricles connect to the third ventricle via the foramina of Monro.

6.98 The lentiform nucleus consists of the caudate nucleus and the globus pallidus.

6.99 The insular lobe consists of the long and short oblique gyri and the limen insula.

6.100 In the thalamus the anterior portion consists mainly of the pulvinar nuclei.

6.101 There are five distinct components of the hippocampal formation.

6.102 The indusium griseum lies on the superior surface of the caudate nucleus.

6.103 Magnetic resonance imaging (MRI) studies in autism have shown maldevelopment of the vermal neocerebellum.

6.104 Obesity may result from over-functioning of lateral nucleus in the mamillary region of hypothalamus.

6.105 Emotional behavioural control is one of the characteristic functions of the mamillary bodies.

6.106 Inorganic lead compounds do not tend to cause acute encephalopathy in adults.

6.107 Functional neuroimaging studies in dementia have shown decreased phospomonoesterases in Alzheimer's disease.

6.108 In Parkinson's disease, the least likely finding in the substantia nigra is degeneration of dopaminergic neurones in the pars reticulata.

6.109 Cerebrospinal fluid levels of bombesin are found to be increased in individuals with schizophrenia.

6.110 The central nervous system is of endodermal origin.

6.111 Conduction in the generator potential is passive and does not summate.

6.112 H_3 receptors that are exclusively located on pre-synaptic axon terminals inhibit the release of a variety of neurotransmitters.

6.113 The target cell will hyperpolarise if the transmitter substance binds to a ligand-gated receptor that admits small positive ions into the cell.

6.114 In electromyography studies of sleep, bipolar recording measures muscle tone in the submental facial muscles.

6.115 The Na^+ equilibrium potential in the neuronal membrane is +66 mV.

6.116 Taurine depresses neuronal excitability by means of synaptic signalling.

6.117 'Sham rage' refers to features seen when rage is induced in experimental animals.

6.118 Dopamine D_1 antagonists can block long-term potentiation.

6.119 In schizophrenia the adrenocorticotrophic hormone (ACTH) release of cortisol from the adrenal cortex is blunted.

6.120 The paraventricular nucleus of the hypothalamus exhibits control over production of hormones in both the anterior and posterior pituitary.

6.121 The muscarinic receptor subtype that stimulates phosphatidylinositol (PI) is implicated in the learning process.

6.122 The inhibitory neuropeptide galanin causes a marked increase in food intake, particularly evoking a preference for fats over carbohydrates.

6.123 The *demethylation hypothesis of schizophrenia* is based on the fact that hallucinogens such as mescaline are often demethylated versions of catecholamines such as dopamine.

6.124 Experiment studies have suggested that individuals who sustain a persistent cortisol elevation for up to twenty hours after exercise may be prone to memory deficits.

6.125 Biological differences in persons with pre-menstrual syndrome compared with those in normal persons are found in both the follicular and luteal cycles.

6.126 In hormone receptors linked to a G protein that lead eventually to the activation of an enzyme, the G protein consists of three subunits each of which is bound in the resting state to guanosine diphosphate (GDP).

6.127 Proglumide is a cholecystokinin-8 antagonist.

6.128 *Illusion de sosies* is commonly associated with right frontotemporal dysfunction.

6.129 Follicle stimulating hormone binds to specific receptors on corpus luteum cells to increase the production of testosterone.

6.130 Glutamate is a precursor of γ-aminobutyric acid (GABA), and both act as inhibitory neurotransmitters in the central nervous system.

6.131 Dopaminergic receptors coupled to G proteins include the D2-like receptors that are negatively coupled via Gi to adenylate cyclase.

6.132 Post mortem studies of schizophrenia have consistently shown an increased density of *N*-methyl-D-aspartate (NMDA) glutamate receptors.

6.133 The cell bodies of serotonergic neurons are found in the brainstem.

6.134 Tryptophan hydroxylase is the enzyme involved in the rate-determining step of serotonin biosynthesis.

6.135 Decreased cholinergic activity has been associated with depressive disorders.

6.136 Concentrations of 5-hydroxyindoleacetic acid (5-HIAA), in contrast to those of neuropeptide Y, have been found to be reduced in the brains of suicide completers.

6.137 In the catabolism of noradrenaline, vanillyl mandelic acid (VMA) is produced in both the pathway starting with the catechol-*O*-

methyltranferase (COMT) enzyme and that starting with monoamine oxidase (MAO).

6.138 In patients with obsessive-compulsive disorder who have responded to selective serotonin reuptake inhibitors, when their diets are depleted of tryptophan abruptly there is a temporary increase in obsessive-compulsive symptoms.

6.139 Sites of metabolism of drugs include the lung, lymphocytes and adrenal cortex.

6.140 With regard to the rate of absorption of a drug, the Henderson-Hasselbach equation indicates that a drug is fully ionised when the pH is equal to the pKa.

6.141 The major pharmacodynamic effects of caffeine are mediated by its stimulation of adenosine receptors.

6.142 The concentration of a psychotropic drug in breast-milk is approximately 1% that of the drug plasma levels in the mother.

6.143 In positron emission tomography (PET) studies of drug interactions with receptors, free ligand concentration with respect to central dopamine receptor occupation is linear.

6.144 In zero-order elimination, the half-life increases as the plasma concentration of the drug increases.

6.145 Brofaromine is effective in controlling paruresis in social phobia.

6.146 Although there have been very few adverse reports about the use of gabapentin in the treatment of bipolar affective disorder in patients with severe liver disease, valproate is to be preferred since more is known about its use in such patients.

6.147 Phase II trials in drug development involve safety and early clinical pharmacology.

6.148 It is possible to improve the bioavailability of a drug through increasing hepatic blood flow, which would reduce the effect of pre-synaptic elimination.

6.149 Polypharmacy with lithium is associated with decreased chlorpromazine concentration.

6.150 Peak plasma levels of mirtazepine are reached about five hours after oral administration.

6.151 Side-effects of topiramate include ataxia, paraesthesia and weight loss.

6.152 For a drug obeying linear kinetics and being administered at regular intervals, it can be shown that the ratio of maximum plasma concentration to minimum plasma concentration achieved is the same as the ratio of regular dosing interval to the half-life of the drug involved.

6.153 With antipsychotic treatment, a decrease in cerebrospinal fluid (CSF) neurotensin concentration in patients with schizophrenia corresponds to a decrease in psychotic symptoms.

6.154 Most studies have reported the efficacy of mirtazepine to be equivalent to that of amitriptyline in the treatment of depressive disorders.

6.155 Intracavernosal injection of metaraminol is used in the management of drug-induced priapism.

6.156 Peak levels of sodium valproate are achieved in four to six hours.

6.157 If a reasonable possibility exists that a proposed treatment is better than placebo, it is considered ethical to carry out a placebo-controlled study.

6.158 Retrograde ejaculation has been associated with antipsychotic therapy, particularly treatment with trifluoperazine.

6.159 Clonidine, an α_2-agonist, is useful in the treatment of both the somatic and emotional aspects of anxiety.

6.160 Risperidone displays a higher level of plasma protein binding than does sulpiride.

6.161 With regard to the placebo effect, tablets are viewed as less potent than capsules.

6.162 The bioavailability of two different brand name products of a generic drug will not differ by more than about 10%.

6.163 A Robertsonian translocation occurs when chromosomes of two different pairs exchange segments.

6.164 Restriction fragment length polymorphisms (RFLPs) and single-nucleotide polymorphisms (SNPs) may both be used in molecular genetic association studies of psychiatric disorders.

6.165 A *Taq-1* polymorphism at the serotonin receptor $5HT_{2C}$ gene locus has been associated with alcoholism and drug misuse in a number of studies.

6.166 The order of deoxyribonucleic (DNA) fragments in a DNA fragment library is not preserved.

6.167 DeBarsey syndrome is an autosomal recessive disorder.

6.168 In a twin study, the proband-wise concordance rate will be higher than the pair-wise concordance rate.

6.169 *Linkage equilibrium* refers to the situation where two genes are in close proximity in a genome such that any crossing-over occurring between the two sites is uncommon.

6.170 In the study of the genetic contribution of psychiatric disorders, while narrowing the phenotype of the disorder to be investigated tends to improve the chances of determining a genetic abnormality, it is often recommended that one broaden the phenotype of the disorder to be studied.

6.171 Coffin-Lowry Syndrome is an X-linked recessive disorder.

6.172 *Epistasis* is considered to be important in the production of the variability of phenotype seen in patients with fragile X syndrome.

6.173 In logarithm of odds (LOD) score analysis, a LOD score of 5.1 or greater is required before one can state that the linkage is highly significant ($p < 0.001$).

6.174 Myotonic dystrophy, Huntington disease and spinocerebellar ataxia type 1 are all caused by expansions of repeat sequences in a single major locus.

6.175 Family genetic association studies may avail of *trios* where an affected patient is studied along with two of his siblings.

6.176 In population genetics, blood pressure is considered to be an example of a quantitative phenotype.

6.177 The Clinical Anxiety Scale developed by Snaith does not rate the severity of anxiety.

6.178 The statistical significance of difference in means between two or more independent variables may be determined simultaneously by one-way analysis of variance (ANOVA).

6.179 Therapist qualities such as genuineness can be rated on the *Modified Rogers Scale.*

6.180 The likelihood ratio for a negative test result is the likelihood that a negative test comes from a person with the disorder rather than one without the disorder.

6.181 The *Mania State Rating Scale* converts descriptive data into nominal data.

6.182 The Poisson distribution is an example of a continuous probability distribution.

6.183 The *State-Trait Anxiety Inventory* has good inter-rater reliability but has poor test-retest reliability on the state scale.

6.184 Probability is an expression of the degree of belief that a particular outcome will occur.

6.185 The *Hamilton Rating Scale for Depression* has a stable factor analytical structure.

6.186 In evidence-based medicine, cohort studies are generally consider-ed to provide higher quality evidence than case-control studies.

6.187 *Construct validity* is based on an accumulation of related validity studies made over time.

6.188 Feighner's Criteria describe twelve psychiatric disorders.

6.189 Depending on the test used, *degree of freedom* relates to the number of subjects.

6.190 The Wilcoxon signed rank sum test is generally used on paired data drawn from a non-Normal distribution.

6.191 Categorical data does not follow logical order.

6.192 An advantage of cohort studies is that the effects of multiple risk factors can be studied.

6.193 The population attributable fraction looks at the impact of an exposure in contrast to its effect.

6.194 Kappa scores are of little benefit in investigating the procedural validity of an instrument.

6.195 According to epidemiologists, the *incubation period* for a single gene disorder is the time from birth until the onset of the disorder.

6.196 In establishing a causal relationship between a disease and a risk factor, *plausibility* as a criterion is not as relevant for newly described diseases in comparison to diseases where there is an accepted body of knowledge.

6.197 A nested cohort study is one that is based within a case-control study.

6.198 The Epidemiologic Catchment Area (ECA) Program employed a study design that used lay interviewers trained to use the Structured Clinical Instrument for DSM-III (SCID) on an adult population in five centres in the USA.

6.199 A trauma happening to an individual is, in epidemiological terms, a necessary but not sufficient cause for post-traumatic stress disorder.

6.200 *Overmatching* is one technique whereby the effects of potential confounders in a case-control study may be reduced and thus increasing the power of the study.

Answers to Question Papers

Answers to Question Paper 1: Clinical Topics

1.1   **False.** According to the St. Louis group, Briquet's hysteria is confined to women. **[B. p495]**

1.2   **True.** Disorientation, diminished concentration and difficulty with simple tests of cognitive function may also be seen. **[PP. p168]**

1.3   **False. [XX. p252]**

1.4   **True.** This involves allowing patients to experience and become accustomed to physical symptoms that increase their anxiety, e.g. getting the patient to hyperventilate to bring on dizziness/para-aesthesia. **[VV. p819]**

1.5   **True. [NN. p2323]**

1.6   **True.** The ratio of male to female varies from near equivalence to 2:1. **[VV. p1943]**

1.7   **False.** It has an equal sex incidence. **[CF. p427]**

1.8   **False.** It was written by Juliet Mitchell. **[AJ. p154]**

1.9   **False.** They argued that elderly relinquish social roles in preparation for death. **[AE. p30]**

1.10 **True.** It is rare in adults and is associated with rheumatic fever in children. **[C. p1087]**

1.11 **True.** It is more common among the elderly. **[B. p754]**

1.12 **False.** It should always be drawn up in consultation with the patient and carer. **[AK. p73]**

1.13 **False.** They are affected only in higher doses. **[NN. p807]**

1.14 **True.** The age period of 10–30 is the time of most self-injurious behaviour in this population. **[VV. p1974]**

1.15 **False.** Research has shown that it has a better outcome than other subtypes. **[B. p434]**

1.16 **False.** The figure is somewhat lower: 5–7%. **[AC. p143]**

1.17 **True. [B. p807]**

1.18 **True.** Since the latter has a number of somatic items that can be confounded by physical illness. **[N. p13]**

1.19 **True. [B. p736]**

1.20 **False.** The opposite is true. **[H. p66]**

1.21 **False.** From a lesion in the frontal convexity. **[NN. p182]**

1.22 **True.** Although such impairment will obviously be frequently present, it is not commonly explicitly required for diagnosis. **[VV. p1689]**

1.23 **True. [B. p342]**

1.24 **False. [C. p658]**

1.25 **True. [NN. p2210]**

1.26 **False.** This was true only of trained researchers; clinicians had a κ-score of 0.30. **[VV. p1687]**

1.27 **False.** Infanticide is the commonest. **[B. p817]**

1.28 **True.** Almost invariably patients are able to name the watch and pen. **[AE. p155]**

1.29 **False.** In structural family therapy. **[LL. p212]**

1.30 **True.** Also in de Lange syndrome and Lesch-Nyhan syndrome. **[YY. p77]**

1.31 **True. [PP. p471]**

1.32 **False.** This is an often misquoted finding. The correct conclusion is that the incidence of broadly defined schizophrenia varied by a factor of four. **[AO. p13]**

1.33 **False.** The opposite is true. **[B. p510]**

1.34 **True.** Patients also tend to recover consciousness more quickly from the former. **[PP. p250]**

1.35 **False.** The onset is usually sudden, while one third are simple. Human forms predominate in the complex group. **[CF. p427]**

1.36 **False.** The opposite is true. **[AK. p117]**

1.37 **True. [B. p333]**

1.38 **True.** However patients are less likely to act out on more dangerous command hallucinations. **[VV. p2044]**

1.39 **True.** Decreased beta activity occurs in the very old. **[U. p403]**

1.40 **True. [AL. p65]**

1.41 **False. [NN. p 213]**

1.42 **False.** It is axis IV in the ICD-10 multiaxial system. **[VV. p1688]**

1.43 **True.** [Smith I, Hillman A. *Mangement of Alcohol Korsakoff Syndrome.* **Advances in Psychiatric Treatment** 1999; 5: 271–8.]

1.44 **False.** The opposite is true. **[B. p613]**

1.45 **False.** The opposite is true. **[JJ. p355–6]**

1.46 **True.** Hyperschemazia refers to an increased awareness and sensation of some parts of one's body. **[H. p235]**

1.47 **True. [AC. p17]**

1.48 **True. [H. p69]**

1.49 **True. [NN. p2349]**

1.50 **False.** The higher rate of disorders among boys during childhood is reversed in adolescence because of the high rates of internalising disorders among girls. **[VV. p1698]**

1.51 **True.** Methadone overdose can have an unpredictable course. **[B. p357]**

1.52 **False.** It was first used in 1879 to describe the emotional damage caused by a railway accident without any obvious physical pathology. **[AN. p80]**

1.53 **False.** This is the professional obligation. **[NN. p2760]**

1.54 **False.** The child is usually sitting up in bed. **[AC. p100]**

1.55 **True. [U. p397]**

1.56 **True.** Although further studies are required to confirm this. **[X. p484]**

1.57 **True.** The increase is six times higher in females. **[B. p811]**

1.58 **False.** Punishment can sometimes be seen in this way; over-correction refers to getting the child to correct the behaviour and then do something else related to make amends. **[AC. p189]**

1.59 **False.** Only FRAXA shows anticipation. **[B. p619]**

1.60 **True.** Possible explanations are increased alienation in winter or intrinsic annual changes in biological rhythms. **[C. p514]**

1.61 **False.** This is characteristic of Pick's disease. **[AE. p95]**

1.62 **False.** It is associated with hypercalcaemia. **[YY. p74]**

1.63 **False.** They have relatively good verbal memory and reading. **[CD. p382]**

1.64 **True.** Research supports this finding, especially when there is an associated movement disorder. [McDonald DGM, McMenamin JB. *Moving beyond Birth Asphyxia as the cause of Cerebral Palsy.* **Irish Medical Journal** 2001; 94(3): 68–70.]

1.65 **True.** It refers to nervous system accommodation. **[NN. p777]**

1.66 **True.** As is childhood disintegrative psychosis. **[YY. p91]**

1.67 **False.** Jung was biased against group therapy. **[CJ. p85]**

1.68 **True. [V. p371]**

1.69 **False.** The opposite is true. **[NN. p2328]**

1.70 **True.** Since euphoria is absent in a proportion of manic episodes in the elderly. **[N. p40]**

1.71 **True.** These are bizarre necrotic lesions with sharp geometrical outlines that are usually asymmetrical. **[CF. p545]**

1.72 **True. [B. p335]**

1.73 **False.** It was introduced in DSM-III. **[I. p1466]**

1.74 **False.** A dependence syndrome for caffeine is specifically excluded. **[I. p988]**

1.75 **False.** Most suicides were impulsive. **[CF. p555]**

1.76 **False.** It accounts for 75%. **[AO. p13]**

1.77 **True. [NN. p1628]**

1.78 **False.** It was increased two-fold in London. **[AC. p70]**

1.79 **True. [CG. p456]**

1.80 **True. [C. p16]**

1.81 **True. [B. p311]**

1.82 **True.** One study of 100 subjects found this: a quarter had suicidal ideation. **[VV. p2085]**

1.83 **False.** It is a variant of the strategic model. **[CJ. p242]**

1.84 **True. [AP. p144]**

1.85 **True.** Less than 50 is normal, while more than 200 leads to fragile X syndrome. **[NN. p2216]**

1.86 **False.** The time taken for depots to reach steady state is about three months. **[C. p411]**

1.87 **False.** Generalised anxiety disorder increases in prevalence with age. **[U. p422]**

1.88 **False.** They refer to insanity. **[AQ. p341]**

1.89 **True. [NN. p2215]**

1.90 **True.** There is a progression of use in this from beer/wine first, then cigarettes, then cannabis leading on finally to other drug use. **[AD. p20]**

1.91 **False.** Not the mother herself but the breast; later in development the mother becomes the object. **[B. p852]**

1.92 **True. [V. p39]**

1.93 **False.** For infants between 1 month and 1 year. **[B. p677]**

1.94 **False.** While this is thought to be a predictor of good outcome in the elderly, it is also thought to be a predictor of poor outcome in younger patients. **[AE. p555]**

1.95 **True.** On SPECT scanning some patients with Alzheimer's disease show anterior rather than posterior hypoperfusion. **[PP. p465]**

1.96 **False. [B. p489]**

1.97 **True.** As the motivation is complex. **[B. p819]**

1.98 **False.** Russell *et al.* found that this was the case only for those under 18 and who had the illness for a relatively short time.

[**C. p877**]

1.99   **False.** While the sensitivity is lower, the specificity is similar. [Drummond C, Ghodse H. *Use of investigations in the diagnosis and management of alcohol use disorders.* **Advances in Psychiatric Treatment** 1999; 5: 366–73.]

1.100 **False.** Although this is the case in ICD-10, in DSM-IV they are grouped under the general heading of 'sexual and gender identity disorders'. [**X. p486**]

1.101 **True.** [**AE. p27**]

1.102 **True.** This rises to 20–45% in those treated for over a year. [**AD. p61**]

1.103 **False.** Approximately 25%. [**B. p672**]

1.104 **True.** [**C. p280**]

1.105 **False.** Only until he elicits a desired response. [**B. p545**]

1.106 **False.** Both have been found useful; massed practice is the deliberate repetition of the tic. [**AC. p172**]

1.107 **True.** Except that the changes are more severe in multi-infarct dementia. [**PP. p454**]

1.108 **False.** The opposite is true. [**YY. p212**]

1.109 **False.** Only two of them: current absence of a confiding relationship and loss of the mother before the age of eleven are of key importance in attachment theory. [**LL. p235**]

1.110 **True.** The apathy seen in many acute brain syndromes tends to lead to diminished aggression, although the patient may be more irritable. [**H. p331**]

1.111 **True.** [**AP. p26**]

1.112 **True.** [**C. p42**]

1.113 **False.** [**AE. p97**]

1.114 **True.** In families where there are at least four children. [**AC. p47**]

1.115 **False.** D'Elia electrode placement position is recommended. [**CL. p25**]

1.116 **False.** The opposite is true. [**C. p1247**]

1.117 **True.** This may lower the risk of coronary heart disease but the risk of breast cancer needs to be taken into consideration. [**B. p335**]

1.118 **True.** Other attitudes in society that are associated with lower rates of alcoholism include: drinking is seen as neither sinful nor virtuous, abstinence is permissible and drinking to excess is not acceptable. [**AD. p114**]

1.119 True. Psychomotor retardation and delusions! **[II. p400]**

1.120 False. Unresolved affective loss and guilt are believed to be the underlying problems. **[AR. p476]**

1.121 True. [NN. p2218]

1.122 True. Although the prevalence is obviously less common than in the abuser. **[XX. p28]**

1.123 False. [Muir WJ. *Genetics advances and learning disability.* **British Journal of Psychiatry** 2000; 176: 12–18.]

1.124 False. She asserted that all early embryos are female. **[AS. p116]**

1.125 False. The beneficial effects are long lasting (for a week) in the latter procedure as well. **[JJ. p274]**

1.126 True. For example, if coercion is used to obtain consent. **[XX. p34]**

1.127 False. In vitro not in vivo. **[U. p393]**

1.128 True. [AT. p144]

1.129 False. It does not include aphasia. **[PP. p65–7]**

1.130 True. Most suicide behaviour occurs in the first six months after diagnosis. **[PP. p330]**

1.131 True. [CF. p425]

1.132 False. It refers to the fact that over-investment in absolute abstinence may itself contribute to the catastrophic nature of relapse when it occurs. **[AD. p41]**

1.133 True. [NN. p2353]

1.134 True. The frequencies given for this population were 5.9% and 2.4 % respectively. **[C. p765]**

1.135 True. Two therapists is the minimum number for the work. **[CE. p237]**

1.136 False. The opposite is true for reasons that are unclear. **[BF. p132]**

1.137 False. This is a recognised but not a common complication. **[NN. p2364]**

1.138 True. As is inappropriate affect. **[L. p86]**

1.139 True. [CI. p185]

1.140 False. This is one of the areas of cognitive deficiency and distortion in aggressive children. **[AC. p191]**

1.141 False. The patient cannot bar such information in this circumstance. **[NN. p2761]**

1.142 False. This is the case for lithium; a negative family history may be a predictor of good response to carbamazepine. **[I. p1413]**

1.143 True. It can present with choreiform and dystonic movement disorders and depression. **[PP. p757]**

1.144 False. The opposite is true. **[BT. p184]**

1.145 True. [NN. p171]

1.146 False. A characteristic feature is the way exhibitionists tend to act in the same way: some will expose themselves only in the same place each time. **[H. p250]**

1.147 True. [Moss S, Emerson E, Kiernan C, *et al. Psychiatric symptoms in adults with learning disability and challenging behaviour.* **British Journal of Psychiatry** 2000; 177: 452–6.]

1.148 False. Ambivalence and hostility are believed to underlie the relationship. **[AM. p.188]**

1.149 False. This produces transcortical sensory aphasia, in which repetition is preserved (this distinguishes it from Wernicke's aphasia). **[NN. p189]**

1.150 True. They have an increased risk of affective disorders of about four-fold. **[VV. p1693]**

1.151 True. [U. p424]

1.152 True. [X. p115]

1.153 False. Delinquency is. **[B. p669]**

1.154 True. Thus 10 mg of temazepam is equivalent to 5 mg of diazepam. **[AD. p62]**

1.155 True. [CG. p460]

1.156 False. It is used as an explanation of binge eating. **[C. p888]**

1.157 False. This refers to challenging the formal hospitalisation: this is more common among paranoid patients. **[NN. p2750]**

1.158 False. Higher: 10–15%. **[AE. p574]**

1.159 True. The hypothesis is known as Cartesian Dualism, and was described by Descartes. **[B. p785]**

1.160 True. This refers to translation of thoughts into imagery. **[BC. p48]**

1.161 False. It is a trait marker. **[B. p342]**

1.162 True. He proposed an 'ethnic' classification system. **[I. p2588]**

1.163 False. It occurs in 30%; 70% result from microdeletions. [Muir WJ. *Genetics advances and learning disability.* **British Journal of Psychiatry** 2000; 176: 12–18.]

1.164 False. The deletion occurs on the short arm of chromosome 11. **[BF. p126]**

1.165 False. They are of uncertain validity with the paranoid subtype being the one possible exception. **[X. p259]**

1.166　True. The reverse is true for males. **[I. p1304]**

1.167　True. [PP. p770]

1.168　True. [AR. p262]

1.169　False. This cannot be predicted by measuring cannabis levels either in blood or in urine. **[NN. p813]**

1.170　False. The child's relationships with others outside of the family should be normal. **[B. p691]**

1.171　False. Extrapyramidal side-effects are common in all age groups. The elderly are more prone to acute dystonia. **[AK. p113]**

1.172　True. [H. p215]

1.173　True. [LL. p264]

1.174　False. It is associated with an increased risk of offending in later life. **[VV. p2031]**

1.175　False. [Gowers SG, Harrington RC, Whitton A, *et al. Brief scale for measuring the outcomes of emotional and behavioural disorders in children. Health of the Nation Outcome Scales for Children and Adolescents (HoNOSCA).* **British Journal of Psychiatry** 1999; 174: 413–416.]

1.176　True. This is also true of delusions of control. **[AO. p68]**

1.177　True. [NN. p2219]

1.178　True. Thus the individual takes on tasks or characteristics of the opposite sex, for example the grandmother can be more assertive in family organisation. **[AE. p261]**

1.179　True. [CH. p275]

1.180　False. Dissocial personality disorder, not borderline personality disorder, is included in the spectrum. **[C. p128]**

1.181　False. *Mens rea* (the necessary state of mind) is important to find a person guilty. **[B. p823]**

1.182　False. It is almost 100% as a result of the behavioural phenotype of hyperphagia. **[I. p2595]**

1.183　True. [CI. p80]

1.184　False. One in two is the correct statistic. **[BH. p2]**

1.185　False. In countries like South Korea where there is more rapid economic growth. **[AE. p25]**

1.186　True. Both expressive and receptive language skills are lost: there are EEG changes associated with the seizures. **[X. p688]**

1.187　True. [Gabbard GO. *A neurobiologically informed perspective on psychotherapy.* **British Journal of Psychiatry** 2000; 177, 117–122.]

1.188 False. Accumulation of aluminium contributes to its aetiology. **[AR. p363]**

1.189 False. [AE. p158]

1.190 False. One study in England found that less than half of such individuals believed their crime was linked to their drug use. **[VV. p2079]**

1.191 True. [Kamphuis JH, Emmelkamp PMG. *Stalking – a contemporary challenge for forensic and clinical psychiatry.* **British Journal of Psychiatry** 2000; 176: 206–209.]

1.192 False. They do as well as those with more typical obsessional symptoms. **[X. p45]**

1.193 True. It refers to the opioid withdrawal state. **[NN. p850]**

1.194 False. Denial and enabling. Codependence refers to the behavioural responses of the family of the addicted individual. **[I. p948]**

1.195 True. [CL. p25]

1.196 False. It refers to HIV dementia. **[AD. p213]**

1.197 True. By 50%. **[B. p361]**

1.198 True. Although monitoring for side-effects should be meticulous, in particular for hypertension associated with high-dose therapy. **[I. p3091]**

1.199 False. Sequential stages. **[P. p214]**

1.200 False. IgA is deficient in this syndrome. **[V. p301]**

Answers to Question Paper 2: Clinical Topics

2.1   True. [B. p502]

2.2   True. This may be experienced as seeing an object even after it has been removed from the field of vision. [PP. p379]

2.3   False. There are conflicting studies but most authors agree that there is no difference. [B. p575]

2.4   False. [Oyebode F, Brown N, Barry L. *Clinical governance in practice*. **Advances in Psychiatric Treatment**. 1999; 5: 399–404]

2.5   False. One person lives for the welfare of a significant person, neglecting his own life. [NN. p1607]

2.6   True. Since there appears to be two groups of responders: those who respond within the first two weeks, and those who respond at 6–8 weeks. [C. p208]

2.7   True. [B. p199]

2.8   True. This is led by social services whereas the case programme approach (CPA) is led by health services. [AK. p76]

2.9   True. [B. p512]

2.10   False. One study found that alcohol intake was associated with later memory impairment. [PP. p179]

2.11   True. [CF. p71]

2.12   False. [Baldwin R. *Aetiology of late life depression*. **Advances in Psychiatric Treatment** 1999; 5: 435–442]

2.13   False. In DSM-IV. [NN. p1635]

2.14   True. Induction of a panic attack in this manner may be used in behavioural treatment of the disorder. [C. p602]

2.15   True. They are slow to replicate and show pathological effects. [PP. p317]

2.16   False. Lipofuscin is deposited [AU. p90]

2.17   False. Negative view of others is not part of the cognitive triad. [NN. p1851]

2.18   True. Patients with GAD may still respond to buspirone, while this is less likely in patients with panic disorder. [I. p1495]

2.19   False. Not feelings of helplessness: see Endicott's criteria (1984).

[AP. p39]

2.20 **True.** One study has reported this. **[I. p1236]**

2.21 **False.** Only in the acute phase. **[X. p251]**

2.22 **False.** The most common is impotence despite largely normal desire. **[PP. p388–389]**

2.23 **False.** Over 50% develop psychiatric morbidity. **[AP. p 57]**

2.24 **True.** [Johnson RT, Gibbs Jr. CJ. *Creutzfeld-Jacob Disease and Related Transmissible Spongiform Encephalopathies.* **New England Journal of Medicine** 1998; 339: 1994–2004.]

2.25 **False.** Puerperal mania is associated with this. **[X. p223]**

2.26 **False.** One should include it in the differential diagnosis, but the delirious patient with nicotinic acid deficiency tends to be agitated in contrast to the delirium of Wernicke's disease. **[C. p1118–9]**

2.27 **True. [PP. p700]**

2.28 **True.** [Leff J. *Needs of the families of people with schizophrenia.* **Advances in Psychiatric Treatment.** 1998; 4: 277]

2.29 **False.** A recent study from China reported the highest female suicidal rates in the world. **[CK. p41]**

2.30 **True.** Resolution therapy seeks to see if such actions or utterances from the patient can be interpreted as their trying to make sense of their environment or an attempt at conveying their needs. **[N. p275]**

2.31 **False.** The three per week ECT schedule has most cognitive side-effects. It is the treatment of choice where rapid response is crucial. **[CL. p33]**

2.32 **False.** This is another term for voyeurism. **[X. p504]**

2.33 **True. [B. p578]**

2.34 **True.** Suggesting that younger individuals found other means of self-harm. **[AE. p564]**

2.35 **True.** Varimax is the commonest method for rotating variables in psychiatry. **[B. p185]**

2.36 **True. [AR. p121]**

2.37 **True. [B. p343]**

2.38 **False.** It tends to occur in stages 3 and 4. **[C. p1208]**

2.39 **True.** Bromocriptine and dantrolene have been used empirically, although there is no direct evidence for their use as NMS has an unknown aetiology. **[AK. p25]**

2.40 **False.** An increased rate of blinking is seen but this is reduced by administration of a neuroleptic. **[AK. p81]**

2.41   **True. [X. p263]**

2.42   **False.** While most disorders are categorised under the relevant affective category, ICD-10 includes a section for disorders of '...the puerperium not classified elsewhere'. **[C. p911]**

2.43   **False.** Alcohol misuse is a risk factor for the first year. Hopelessness and parasuicide remain risk factors. **[CL. p37]**

2.44   **True.** Both refer to neurotic, as distinct from delusional, jealousy. **[AM. p35]**

2.45   **False. [NN. p222]**

2.46   **True.** Suggesting that consumption of alcohol even in problem drinkers declines with age. **[AE. p673]**

2.47   **True.** Fine spongiform changes are noticed in frontal/temporal areas. **[PP. p465]**

2.48   **False.** Only a minority have a diagnosis of a mental illness. **[AK. p121]**

2.49   **False.** Multivariate analysis did not support this. **[AE. p520]**

2.50   **False.** 'Apraxia' should read 'apathy'. **[N. p13]**

2.51   **True.** This has been quoted in several studies. [Wieck A, Kumar R, Hirst AD. *Increased sensitivity of dopamine receptors and recurrence of affective psychosis after childbirth.* **British Medical Journal** 1991; 303: 613–616.]

2.52   **False.** The primary cause is asphyxiation. **[BW. p71]**

2.53   **True.** Negative symptoms without positive ones are sufficient to arrive at this diagnosis. **[X. p261]**

2.54   **False.** It is more in the region of 10–20%. **[N. p29]**

2.55   **True. [CL. p28]**

2.56   **False.** The risk of developing Alzheimer's disease is increased three-fold for heterozygotes carrying the ε4 allele. **[BH. p60]**

2.57   **False.** 60%. **[AE. p529]**

2.58   **True.** This is also known as 'body sway'; an increased latency in the P300 event-related potential has also been reported in this population. **[AD. p100]**

2.59   **True.** It is similar to hallucinogenic drugs in this respect. **[B. p360]**

2.60   **False.** It is more common in girls than in boys. **[B. p670]**

2.61   **True.** DSM-IV criteria give more stress to the importance of course and impairment. **[X. p257]**

2.62   **False.** ICD-10 rules out a diagnosis of generalised anxiety disorder if one meets the full criteria for a depressive episode. **[N. p141]**

2.63   **False. [CL. p25]**

2.64 **False.** An alteration in this aspect of self-awareness is what occurs in passivity experiences. **[V. p21]**

2.65 **True.** Durkheim's social theory explains the spring seasonal peak of suicide as increased interpersonal conflict and to excess alcohol consumption. **[CK. p24]**

2.66 **True.** It is listed in DSM-IV as one of the ten signs of tobacco withdrawal. **[I. p929]**

2.67 **False.** Non-Hodgkin's lymphoma is the commonest and occurs in 2–6% of patients. **[PP. p321]**

2.68 **True. [C. p591]**

2.69 **True.** A well-designed Finnish study reported the suicide rate in schizophrenia was 7% and in personality disorders was 31%. **[CK. p172]**

2.70 **False.** This gene is linked to familial Alzheimer's disease, but the gene responsible for Alzheimer's in the Volga German descendants is the *STM2* gene on chromosome 1. **[AE. p129]**

2.71 **False.** 30–50% have the outcome described; the others have deficits that are relatively static. **[PP. p327]**

2.72 **False.** This has been found by Caine. **[C. p1016]**

2.73 **False.** With δ-opioid receptors. **[NN. p845]**

2.74 **False.** The commonest emotional response is anger. **[A. p730]**

2.75 **True.** It may be used in the treatment of nocturnal enuresis, and has a lower rate of side-effects than do the tricyclics. **[II. p386]**

2.76 **True. [B. p299]**

2.77 **False.** They have this dubious honour according to the World Drink Trends Survey 2002. [Sommerland N. *The Irish Mirror* 17/12/01 (a sadly neglected resource for those preparing for the MRCPsych).]

2.78 **True.** Dynorphin can act to diminish the excessive dopaminergic activity. **[I. p974]**

2.79 **True. [AC. p16]**

2.80 **True. [C. p591]**

2.81 **True. [NN. p181]**

2.82 **False.** Since the presentation and course of OCD in both adults and children is similar; depressive disorder on the other hand may be used as an example. **[VV. p1685]**

2.83 **False.** Familial inheritance is autosomal dominant. **[PP. p751]**

2.84 **True. [C. p887]**

2.85 **False.** Doctors need to be trained as well. **[B. p332]**

2.86   **False.** It is a structured interview. **[AD. p9]**

2.87   **True.** If that person was too drunk to form an intent. **[V. p263]**

2.88   **True. [C. p788]**

2.89   **False.** It slightly improves this. **[NN. p2330]**

2.90   **False.** Other factors such as impulsivity or whether the patient is in accord with the goal have been found to be more important indicators. **[AD. p13]**

2.91   **True. [P. p52]**

2.92   **True. [AL. p94]**

2.93   **True. [B. p303]**

2.94   **False.** The avoidance of arguments is one of the central strategies in this technique. **[AD. p163]**

2.95   **True.** [Turner S. _Psychiatric help for survivors of torture._ **Advances in Psychiatric Treatment** 2000; 6: 295–303.]

2.96   **False.** _Civilisation and Its Discontents._ **[AZ. p160–1]**

2.97   **False.** Lack of empathy. **[B. p663]**

2.98   **True.** Other areas are also tested such as use of knowledge and spatial imaging. **[AC. p91]**

2.99   **True.** [Hall I. _Young offenders with a learning disability._ **Advances in Psychiatric Treatment** 2000; 6: 278–285.]

2.100 **False.** He felt this was the case with catharsis. **[BC. p48]**

2.101 **False.** Although this depends upon the definition, around 10% of children suffer from obesity. **[B. p674]**

2.102 **False.** Although 'much more' is obviously a subjective term, paranoid delusions are only slightly more common in these patients. The incidences are roughly: 80% versus 60–70% respectively. **[I. p978]**

2.103 **True.** Xanthenes and neuroleptics are also associated with it. **[CE. p127]**

2.104 **False.** This statement refers to verbal paraphasia. **[H. p167]**

2.105 **True. [AE. p27]**

2.106 **True.** Those who do develop speech usually have marked delays in developing both understanding and expressive language skills. **[AC. p106]**

2.107 **False.** Onset is usually in middle age/old age; the course can be intermittent over many years. **[PP. p678]**

2.108 **True.** In vascular dementia somatic complaints are common. **[AE. p462]**

2.109 **False.** Around 1%. **[B. p694]**

2.110 True. They are very uncommon in the former but may be seen in the latter. **[AC. p128, 164]**

2.111 False. [CL. p72]

2.112 False. This describes autotopagnosia. **[U. p93]**

2.113 False. On delusions. **[B. p811]**

2.114 True. Although some have argued it may be as high as 3%. **[I. p2592]**

2.115 True. [P. p179]

2.116 False. A profession-based standard exists. **[AX. p314]**

2.117 True. [AE. p31]

2.118 False. The predicted figure is closer to 40%. **[VV. p1693]**

2.119 True. The particular community or culture has to be taken into consideration when deciding who is disabled. **[YY. p27]**

2.120 True. Note that technically, the College can ask a question regarding any of the mental health acts in Great Britain or the Republic of Ireland, although a question such as this one is highly unlikely. **[CU. p284]**

2.121 False. It does refer to present functioning. **[NN. p2208]**

2.122 True. The mice exhibit learning difficulties in several modalities: visual, spatial and attendant learning difficulties. **[I. p2594]**

2.123 False. Reality orientation has been researched but validation therapy has not. **[B. p723]**

2.124 True. Since the latter can be associated with a small steps gait (these are usually rapid however). **[AE. p171]**

2.125 True. But diffuse senile plaques are seen. **[AE. p93]**

2.126 False. The reverse is the case. **[B. p688]**

2.127 False. The GDS is used for that purpose. The Cornell Scale is used for assessing depression in dementia. **[B. p721]**

2.128 False. One's treatment approach should be based on existing evidence in the literature. One has to weigh up the risks and benefits of prescribing 'off licence'. [Fraser B. *Psychopharmacology and people with learning disability.* **Advances in Psychiatric Treatment** 2000; 5: 471–7.]

2.129 True. The prevalence of depressive disorder is 10–40%. **[AE. p346]**

2.130 False. It may be contraindicated in such situations. **[X. p679]**

2.131 True. [B. p580]

2.132 True. [AC. p33]

2.133 False. Use of community resource skills has been described but not

occupational skills. **[NN. p2209]**
2.134 True. Which in turn is related to the number of CGG triplet repeats in the gene. **[I. p2595]**
2.135 False. pH increases. **[U. p398]**
2.136 True. This is referred to as scapegoating. **[AC. p219]**
2.137 False. The second most common: its prevalence is 1 in 15000. **[NN. p2217]**
2.138 False. This will be one of the areas that the court will be most interested in. **[XX. p148–9]**
2.139 False. It is a support group for the teenage children of alcoholics. **[B. p355]**
2.140 False. Existentialism gives priority to phenomenology and ontology. **[CI. p52]**
2.141 False. MRI detects the distribution of the angioma whereas CT detects calcification. **[NN. p2222]**
2.142 False. Less than 1%. **[XX. p29]**
2.143 True. [Bateman AW, Fonagy P. _Effectiveness of psychotherapeutic treatment of personality disorder._ **British Journal of Psychiatry** 2000; 177: 138–143.]
2.144 False. Around 10%: they are 2–3 times more vulnerable than other people with learning disability. **[YY. p144.]**
2.145 True. [AE. p518]
2.146 False. Both have an I.Q. less than 70 as a criterion. **[I. p2589]**
2.147 True. In his book: _Leonardo da Vinci and a Memory of his Childhood._ **[JJ. p65]**
2.148 True. However, they may contribute to violence in the presence of delusions. **[AO. p68]**
2.149 True. [B. p359]
2.150 True. Voluntary false confessions are common in depression. **[B. p822]**
2.151 True. [JJ. p80]
2.152 True. If an individual is touched without consent there is battery. **[AX. p314]**
2.153 True. [NN. p2369]
2.154 False. The latter statistic is correct, but there are roughly 95 causes of X-linked mental retardation recognised. **[I. p2593]**
2.155 False. Most of the evidence for amotivational syndrome comes from uncontrolled studies. [Johns A. _Psychiatric effects of cannabis._ **British Journal of Psychiatry** 2001; 178: 116–122.]

2.156 True. Meaning that the unconscious, like dreams, works through metaphors and signs. **[AJ. p159]**

2.157 False. William's syndrome does not show anxiety symptoms at all. **[NN. p2226]**

2.158 False. Although it is in the rest, is not especially noted in Angelman syndrome. **[I. p2596]**

2.159 False. Greater than twenty-four hours. [Ashton CH. *Pharmacology and effects of cannabis: a brief review.* **British Journal of Psychiatry** 2001; 178: 101–106.]

2.160 False. It is fear of retaliation by the father. **[B. p850]**

2.161 True. In 5% of children this can persists after two years. **[NN. p2361]**

2.162 False. This is true for mild mental retardation: a cause can be identified in around 80% with severe forms. **[VV. p1947]**

2.163 False. All of these with the exception of amphetamines (Class B). **[U. p236]**

2.164 True. [NN. p169]

2.165 True. [NN. p2369]

2.166 True. As hypnogogic hallucinations. **[H. p96]**

2.167 False. It is a comprehensive reading assessment. **[B. p659]**

2.168 False. Kohut described narcissistic rage. **[CI. p151]**

2.169 False. By Fraiberg, in which the parent and child are seen together. **[LL. p197]**

2.170 False. This is an example of secondary prevention: rubella immunization is an example of a primary prevention. **[VV. p1951]**

2.171 True. [H. p89]

2.172 True. In fact of all types of agnosia **[NN. p174]**

2.173 False. The results are contradicting. **[LL. p231]**

2.174 True. [NN. p2209]

2.175 False. It measures the attachments of the adult that were developed as a child. **[P. p205]**

2.176 True. [H. p196]

2.177 True. [B. p693]

2.178 False. The affective instability in this condition is incongruent. **[NN. p169]**

2.179 False. They have a similar prevalence to the general population. **[XX. p254]**

2.180 False. Intrusions are late recurrence of words or thoughts from an earlier context whereas perseveration is inappropriate continuation of an act or thought. **[NN. p169]**

2.181 True. This does not reflect the true intent of the offender. **[B. p809]**

2.182 False. In 1983 it was only twice that of general population. **[NN. p2212]**

2.183 False. Only a minority suffer from a psychiatric illness. **[XX. p260]**

2.184 True. This is not the case with lithium. **[YY. p221]**

2.185 True. [B. p813]

2.186 True. [NN. p2219]

2.187 True. This is what R.D. Laing felt that people with psychosis lacked and which caused them to become psychotic. **[CI. p121]**

2.188 False. One study has shown an unusually high rate. **[V. p82]**

2.189 True. [NN. p2769]

2.190 False. Posterior superior right temporal lobe lesions. **[NN. p174]**

2.191 False. It describes partial responsibility from age 10–14 years. **[U. p430]**

2.192 True. This is associated with a slight paternal age effect. **[BF. p122]**

2.193 False. This refers to the lack of agreed terms to name the factors in the five-factor model. **[JJ. p280]**

2.194 True. [LL. p200]

2.195 True. This explains why the degree of learning disability increases through the generations. **[B. p616]**

2.196 False. Unlike the tort of negligence. **[CU. p290]**

2.197 True. The legal concept of automatism differs from the clinical concept, hence the confusion. **[B. p824]**

2.198 True. [JJ. p331–2]

2.199 True. [C. p90]

2.200 True. One third of cases with infantile spasms show autistic behaviour and one in six meet the criteria for autism. **[BG. p81]**

Answers to Question Paper 3: Clinical Topics

3.1   **False.** NPT is significantly androgen sensitive. **[B. p531]**
3.2   **False.** The so-called 'epileptic dementia' is generally associated with marked personality changes. **[PP. p264]**
3.3   **True.** Partly as a result of greater rates of psychiatric illness in the elderly. **[CK. p280]**
3.4   **False.** No such difference has been reported. **[B. p314]**
3.5   **True. [B. p349]**
3.6   **False.** Over 90% do: these changes can be seen even in patients who demonstrated no neurological signs or symptoms before death. **[PP. p319]**
3.7   **False.** Psychogenic pain is often relieved by alcohol or psychotropic medication. **[CF. p542]**
3.8   **True. [B. p304]**
3.9   **True. [B. p403t]**
3.10 **False.** The increase is more than twenty-fold; beta amyloid accumulation is increased two-fold. **[PP. p442]**
3.11 **True.** For unlikely events odds have approximately the same value as probability. **[B. p200]**
3.12 **True.** This is an historical example of dissociation disorder (conversion hysteria). **[C. p693]**
3.13 **True.** Studies have reported raised levels of Epstein-Barr virus titre. **[NN. p1563]**
3.14 **True.** Any changes in the EEG in Pick's disease, if present, tend to be mild. **[PP. p461]**
3.15 **False.** A stable pattern of suicide has been recorded in Northern Ireland from 1969 to 1987. **[CF. p560]**
3.16 **True. [B. p313]**
3.17 **False.** It may also lead on to separation thereby complicating the real grief process. **[NN. p1724]**
3.18 **False.** It can be a 'flashback' phenomenon associated with LSD use in which the subject sees changes in the whole of their visual field, so that it appears that he can see the air. **[I. p1021]**

3.19 **False**. It is used for psychotic disorders. **[CF. p57]**

3.20 **True**. **[BL. p152]**

3.21 **False**. A female perpetrator is extremely rare. **[NN. p1736]**

3.22 **True**. There is however an inherent bias in that all studies have been retrospective. **[I. p1115]**

3.23 **False**. The precise nature of the material deposited is unknown, nor is the pathogenesis known. **[PP. p759]**

3.24 **True**. **[CK. p194]**

3.25 **True**. **[U. p278]**

3.26 **True**. Other changes in the GABA system associated with schizophrenia are: diminished GABA uptake sites in the hippocampus and diminished cortical GABAergic interneurons. **[I. p1143]**

3.27 **True**. **[PP. p756]**

3.28 **False**. It is more common in social classes II and III. **[X. p115]**

3.29 **True**. Lack of insight and auditory hallucinations are. **[X. p249]**

3.30 **False**. This is the W.H.O. consensus statement: for the Royal Colleges of Psychiatrists and General Practitioners, the period is 4–6 months. **[C. p200]**

3.31 **False**. Mental changes usually appear first. **[PP. p745]**

3.32 **False**. Other common causes are diabetic ketoacidosis, cerebral malignancy, hepatic failure and encephalitis. **[C. p962]**

3.33 **True**. **[X. p221]**

3.34 **True**. **[C. p81]**

3.35 **True**. It produces the same significance level. **[B. p186]**

3.36 **False**. This is not the cognitive defect theory. **[AU. p277]**

3.37 **True**. **[X. p216]**

3.38 **True**. It has but it is uncertain whether benefits are sustained. **[I. p1708]**

3.39 **False**. In all reported cases joint disease presents first. **[PP. p425]**

3.40 **True**. A Finnish study found that such a reduced turnover occurred in sons of men with alcohol dependence that exhibited violence. **[BV. p166]**

3.41 **False**. They have more influence on the onset than on the course. **[X. p216]**

3.42 **False**. While this is obviously highly desirable, marked pressure for change from the patient's environment may suffice. **[I. p1758]**

3.43 **True**. [Hofberg K, Brockington IF. *Tokophobia: an unreasoning dread of childbirth: A series of 26 cases.* **British Journal of Psychiatry** 2000; 176: 83–85.]

3.44 **False.** This is true of the tenth edition; the ninth edition includes 140 symptom items. **[C. p307]**

3.45 **False.** But they have fewer admissions for depression. **[X. p212]**

3.46 **True.** Thus suggesting differing pathological processes. **[I. p3039]**

3.47 **False.** It does lower their mood but does not exacerbate their symptoms. [Bell C, Abrams J, Nutt D. *Tryptophan depletion and its implications for psychiatry.* **British Journal of Psychiatry** 2001; 178: 399–405.]

3.48 **False.** White matter hypointensities have not been reported. [Baldwin R. *Aetiology of late life depression.* **Advances in Psychiatric Treatment.** 1999; 5: 435–442]

3.49 **True. [AE. p99]**

3.50 **False.** As with delusional disorder, it probably increases with age in this group. **[I. p2996]**

3.51 **False.** Fatalistic suicide is the opposite of anomic suicide and occurs in societies with oppressive regimes. **[U. p279]**

3.52 **True. [B. p489]**

3.53 **True. [AE. p98]**

3.54 **False.** As with basic attention span, it is affected to little or no degree by ageing. **[I. p3025]**

3.55 **True.** It has been suggested that late-life onset mania has an admixture of depressive features, however the only prospective study disagrees. **[CF. p241]**

3.56 **True.** This response occurs rather than the more usual tachy-cardia. **[C. p630]**

3.57 **True. [AE. p580]**

3.58 **False.** Since this response is diminished in Alzheimer's disease as well. **[I. p3061]**

3.59 **False.** Due to increased resistance a higher seizure stimulus is required for electroconvulsive therapy. **[II. p400]**

3.60 **True. [AU. p266]**

3.61 **True.** Hysterical illness is almost always secondary in old age. **[AE. p591]**

3.62 **False.** For this term to be used there should not be a psychiatric disorder to account for the visual hallucinations. **[A. p731]**

3.63 **False.** Short-term memory does not change. **[U. p395]**

3.64 **False.** In general, the recidivism rate does not decline with time and is highest in violent offenders and those who offend against children. [Lavelle E. *Biology of sexual disorders.* **CNS** 2000; 2: 4]

3.65   **True. [AE. p587]**

3.66   **True.** The quoted study confirmed that incidence rates of dementia increase steeply with age. [Riedel-Heller SG, Busse A, Aurich C, Matschinger H, Angermeyer MC. *Incidence of dementia according to DSM-III-R and ICD-10. Results of the Leipzig Longitudinal Study of the Aged (LEILA75+), Part 2.* **British Journal of Psychiatry** 2001; 179: 255–60.]

3.67   **False.** These attacks should have occurred within a period of about one month. **[GG. p139]**

3.68   **True. [AR. p117]**

3.69   **False.** The non-lonely isolates. **[AE. p606]**

3.70   **True.** This is the avoidant and dependent cluster: they may be more prevalent among the elderly. **[I. p3079]**

3.71   **False.** 5%. **[B. p713]**

3.72   **True.** The relationship is poorly understood. **[V. p151]**

3.73   **True.** Arras used this term to refer to continued biological life without importance to self-feelings. **[AE. p729]**

3.74   **False.** The quoted study found less than 10% had poor outcome, but noted the lack of research on this area. [Johnson I. *Outcome of alcoholism in old age.* **Irish Journal of Psychological Medicine** 2001; 18(4): 125–128.]

3.75   **True. [AK. p112]**

3.76   **True. [AM. p100]**

3.77   **False.** At 12 units per day. **[B. p335]**

3.78   **False.** Up to a week; it begins after 12–24 hours after caffeine cessation. **[AD. p72]**

3.79   **True.** It occurs in 25% of elderly living independently. **[U. p425]**

3.80   **True.** It has been found in the cerebrospinal fluid of healthy individuals. **[AE. p124]**

3.81   **False.** It is lower among those who drink 1–3 units per day. **[B. p335]**

3.82   **False.** ICD-10 advises that harmful use should not be diagnosed when a substance-induced psychotic disorder is present. **[GG. p75]**

3.83   **False.** The EEG shows excess fast wave activity. **[U. p233]**

3.84   **True.** A conformational change is thought to account for the alteration in function. **[AE. p134]**

3.85   **False.** Only 10%. **[B. p337]**

3.86   **True.** This is the case for males: the female occupation groups that show the heaviest drinking patterns are the professional jobs and non-manual occupations. **[AD. p80]**

3.87   **False.** [Smith I, Hillman A. *Mangement of Alcohol Korsakoff Syndrome. Advances in Psychiatric Treatment* 1999; 5: 271–8.]

3.88   **False.** Bilateral frontal pathology is found in most cases. **[C. p974]**

3.89   **False.** This diagnosis can be made whether act is intentional or involuntary or both. **[NN. p2338t]**

3.90   **True.** Also by esterase in the liver. **[I. p1002]**

3.91   **False.** It comes under the heading of 'episodic use'. **[GG. p77]**

3.92   **False.** In the third person. **[AD. p180]**

3.93   **False.** As 'inhibited' and 'disinhibited' sub-types. **[NN. p2355]**

3.94   **False.** Generally, antipsychotics should be avoided; risperidone has been found to increase the intensity of visual flashback phenomena. **[I. p1023]**

3.95   **True.** Sensitisation will occur more with intermittent use. **[I. p1003]**

3.96   **True. [AD. p126]**

3.97   **True. [NN. p2361]**

3.98   **True.** The prevalence of lifetime heroin dependence was 0.4%, peak rates were found in the 35–44 year old group. **[I. p1040]**

3.99   **True.** It has both stimulant and depressant effects. **[T. p514]**

3.100 **True. [AD. p183]**

3.101 **True. [NN. p2379]**

3.102 **False.** The methadone may be abruptly discontinued in this situation where the patient is on low-dose methadone therapy. **[I. p1053]**

3.103 **False.** While in the past this was the case, alcohol consumption among doctors is now the same as the general population average. **[CL. p122]**

3.104 **True.** Pittman described abstinent, ambivalent, permissive and over-permissive cultures. **[AD. p114]**

3.105 **True. [B. p673]**

3.106 **False.** Their review suggested that this gap had widened. **[VV. p1695]**

3.107 **False.** There are no treatment guidelines for using these drugs; they have been suggested as being beneficial. **[B. p359]**

3.108 **True. [B. p740]**

3.109 **True.** After around 15 minutes. **[B. p674]**

3.110 True. Estimates have ranged largely between 15–22%. **[VV. p1697]**

3.111 False. The fourth category is *Preoccupied* not *Resistant/Ambivalent*. **[P. p205]**

3.112 False. This may occur with lead poisoning. **[AU. p414]**

3.113 False. [B. p691]

3.114 True. Although they tend to give less overall information. **[VV. p1701]**

3.115 False. Gilles de la Tourette syndrome is a lifelong disorder. **[V. p287]**

3.116 True. [AT. p124]

3.117 True. Since adult males are involved in a number of teenage pregnancies. **[B. p695]**

3.118 False. Only about 5% will, although up to two-thirds of parents will have some obsessional traits. **[AC. p132]**

3.119 False. [Goodyer IM, Herbert J, Tamplin A, *et al. First-episode major depression in adolescents: Affective, cognitive and endocrine characteristics of risk status and predictors of onset.* **British Journal of Psychiatry** 2000; 176: 142–149.]

3.120 False. It can raise TCA plasma levels by 40–50%. **[C. p179]**

3.121 True. Also of substance abuse. **[B. p810]**

3.122 True. Only one-fifth of cases of enuresis are associated with psychiatric disorder. **[AC. p143]**

3.123 True. However it occurs less in Asperger's syndrome. **[P. p44]**

3.124 True. Hypoxyphilia involves increasing the sensation of orgasm by cutting down one's air supply. **[AV. p254]**

3.125 False. A recent study reported a 1% incidence. **[B. p812]**

3.126 True. As is the *Kiddie Schedule for Affective Disorders and Schizophrenia.* **[B. p687]**

3.127 False. Onset is usually before two years of age. **[CG. p581]**

3.128 True. [Muir WJ. Genetics advances and learning disability. **British Journal of Psychiatry** 2000; 176: 12–18.]

3.129 True. [NN. p2760]

3.130 True. 24% versus 15% of children in these groups show this behaviour. **[B. p660]**

3.131 False. Hypofrontality has been a consistent finding. [Gowers SG, Harrington RC, Whitton A, *et al. Brief scale for measuring the outcomes of emotional and behavioural disorders in children. Health of the Nation Outcome Scales for children and Adolescents (HoNOSCA)* **British**

Journal of Psychiatry 1999; 174: 413–416.]
3.132 **False.** It is a feature of Williams's syndrome, which includes mild mental retardation associated with superficial sociability. **[CD. p413]**
3.133 **False.** Less than five per year. **[B. p825]**
3.134 **False.** Autism takes precedence. **[X. p694]**
3.135 **True. [CH. p185]**
3.136 **False.** He thought that the psychosis led to the development of the learning disability. **[B. p627]**
3.137 **False. [B. p821]**
3.138 **True.** The commonest method of suicide in this population is by hanging using torn sheets. **[VV. p2040]**
3.139 **True. [CH. p372]**
3.140 **False.** Severe learning disability: onset is at less than one year of age. **[YY. p233]**
3.141 **True.** The reported rate varies widely from 4% to 30%. **[B. p820]**
3.142 **False.** This is the figure for those who are the victims of sexual intercourse; up to 10–15%, according to Mullen, experience sexual assault. **[XX. p30]**
3.143 **True. [AC. p160]**
3.144 **True. [B. p660]**
3.145 **True. [B. p818]**
3.146 **True.** The presence of brain damage alone increased the risk 5-fold. **[U. p367]**
3.147 **False.** About 20% have. **[P. p94]**
3.148 **False.** The range is around 10–20%. **[P. p93]**
3.149 **True. [NN. p2210]**
3.150 **False.** About 70% exhibit this. **[U. p370]**
3.151 **True. [P. p110]**
3.152 **False.** These concepts are part of brief therapy. **[AC. p199]**
3.153 **True.** The location is Xp22. **[NN. p2214]**
3.154 **False.** A study in Scotland found it to be associated with social classes IV and V. **[A. p625]**
3.155 **True. [XX. p17]**
3.156 **False.** Therapy focuses on current relationships and eschews aetiological theorising. **[I. p2178]**
3.157 **True.** Obviously you should mention only the former as a valid management strategy in the clinical examination. **[YY. p164]**

3.158 True. This refers to the fact that parents from any social background may have children with 'pathological' learning difficulties. **[A. p621]**

3.159 False. Those of learning disability are included in abnormal homicides. **[XX. p21]**

3.160 True. A parochial question, but it still addresses an important legal theme. One does not need to have any knowledge of the Irish legal system to have a good chance of getting this correct. **[AN. p422]**

3.161 False. Inappropriate social interactions are the least responsive (35% success rate against 60% success rate for distructive behaviours). **[NN. p2229]**

3.162 False. Severe mental retardation often occurs even after surgery that appears successful. **[A. p627]**

3.163 False. [Jamieson E, Butwell M, Taylor P, *et al. Trends in special (high-security) hospitals: 1: Referrals and admissions.* **British Journal of Psychiatry** 2000; 176: 260–265.]

3.164 True. This is one of the McNaughten rules. **[AN. p378]**

3.165 True. [NN. p2237]

3.166 False. The abnormal repeat is the CGG repeat in fragile X. **[VV. p1953]**

3.167 True. [B. p812–813]

3.168 True. [Birmingham L. *Diversion from Custody.* **Advances in Psychiatric Treatment** 2001; 7: 198–207.]

3.169 True. [NN. p2240]

3.170 False. It is based on ICD-10. **[YY. p107]**

3.171 True. [B. p605]

3.172 False. Over the age of 14, full responsibility for a person's criminal acts exists. **[AQ. p339]**

3.173 False. Around 55% to 75%. **[NN. p2213]**

3.174 True. As is the identification and treatment of any physical or psychiatric illnesses. **[YY. p99]**

3.175 False. Younger age correlated strongly with re-offending. The strongest correlation for subsequent offending was previous offending. **[XX. p217]**

3.176 True. [YY. p11]

3.177 True. This is because of caretakers consistently refusing to listen to the child's statements during preschool years. **[LL. p219–22]**

3.178 False. It refers to children not wanting to return to school.

[H. p220–1]

3.179 False. [Hall I. *Young offenders with a learning disability.* **Advances in Psychiatric Treatment** 2000; 6: 278–285.]

3.180 True. He used these terms when outlining ethical issues regarding individuals with learning disability. **[YY. p191]**

3.181 False. No such difference has been reported. **[LL. p250]**

3.182 True. [NN. p177]

3.183 False. In DSM-IV, borderline intellectual functioning appears as a V code. [Chaplin R, Flynn A. *Adults with learning disability admitted to psychiatric wards.* **Advances in Psychiatric Treatment** 2000; 6: 128–134.]

3.184 True. It was developed in *Psychological Factors Determining Human Behaviour.* **[AS. p55]**

3.185 False. No such trend has been reported but maternal loss by death before the age of six is more commonly associated with depression. **[LL. p240]**

3.186 False. The full symptoms only occur with bilateral medial frontal lobe lesions. **[I. p237-8]**

3.187 True. [Guthrie E. *Psychotherapy for patients with complex disorders and chronic symptoms: The need for a new research paradigm.* **British Journal of Psychiatry** 2000; 177: 131–137.]

3.188 True. However, it should be genuine and relevant. **[BA. p165]**

3.189 False. It is always based on operant conditioning concepts. **[A. p25]**

3.190 True. [NN. p190]

3.191 True. Less insightful work may be accomplished through an interpreter. **[I. p2214-5]**

3.192 False. This stage should be allowed to run its course. **[BC. p110]**

3.193 False. According to Tizard, this depends on the family environment. **[A. p65]**

3.194 True. Fawcett *et al* suggested this for depressed patients with anxiety symptoms. **[CK. p188]**

3.195 False. Self-transcendence is one of the three dimensions of character. [Gabbard GO. *A neurobiologically informed perspective on psychotherapy.* **British Journal of Psychiatry** 2000; 177, 117–122.]

3.196 True. [Veale D. *Cognitive-behavioural therapy for body dysmorphic disorder.* **Advances in Psychiatric Treatment** 2001; 7: 125–132.]

3.197 **True.** [**JJ. p445**]

3.198 **False.** Major depression was found to be a late complication of the alcoholism. [**CK. p140–1**]

3.199 **False.** It is an example of ideomotor apraxia. [**U. p92**]

3.200 **False.** It is collecting/hoarding and can occur separately from senile self-neglect. [**B. p742**]

Answers to Question Paper 4: Basic Sciences

4.1   **True.** Parkes reported these findings. **[LL. p273]**

4.2   **False.** They don't, however they prefer their mother's voice to the voices of other women. **[EE. p81]**

4.3   **False.** This is the reverse of the *Social Learning Theory*. According to Kohlberg children attend to the same sex models because they have developed a consistent gender identity. **[G. p196]**

4.4   **False.** This is a method of measuring learning and memory. **[AY. p406]**

4.5   **False.** She reports that attachment theory helps us to understand the early anxieties and fears of a child as legitimate responses to real experiences of maltreatment **[LL. p297]**

4.6   **True.** Thus children at this stage of development feel that moral laws (such as not hitting someone) are as real as the laws of physics (such as gravity). **[EE. p89]**

4.7   **True.** This was described by Chomsky to account for our creativity with language and our intuition regarding the structure of language. **[FF. p69]**

4.8   **False.** Allochiria occurs with spatial neglect. **[AY. p210]**

4.9   **True.** Possibly as the social custom has a divisive rather than supporting continuation. **[LL. p43]**

4.10   **False.** The preoperational stage is considered to be a subperiod by some in contrast to the sensorimotor, concrete operations and formal operations periods. **[I. p403]**

4.11   **False.** The child shows signs of distress when it is separated from its attachment figure. **[U. p26]**

4.12   **False.** The reverse is true. **[BX. p396]**

4.13   **True.** If this behaviour offers the best hope of reproductive success, even though this may be incompatible with psychological well-being, according to attachment theorists. **[LL. p62]**

4.14   **True.** They also prefer warm and soft mother figures to the opposites. **[EE. p100]**

4.15   **False.** This is a definition of gender identity. Gender role is the type of behaviour an individual engages in that identifies them as being either male or female. **[U. p36]**

4.16 **True. [AY. p198]**

4.17 **True.** This occurs as their search for comparable reemployment fails. **[LL. p82]**

4.18 **True.** However Vygotsky felt that these processes affect each other later on in development. **[FF. p75]**

4.19 **True. [QQ. p309]**

4.20 **True.** It was developed by Norman & Shallice. **[AY. p248]**

4.21 **True. [LL. p288]**

4.22 **False.** This was not found in a study that looked at the issue, suggesting that relationship difficulties are not the result of a global difficulty in understanding non-verbal affect. **[FF. p180]**

4.23 **True.** Over repeated pairings the second drug may come to alter the effect of the first. **[FF. p25]**

4.24 **False.** This is the *phi phenomenon*. **[AY. p213]**

4.25 **False.** Seligman postulated that the psychogenesis of depression depends on the individual's beliefs rather than his situation. **[LL. p276]**

4.26 **False.** Other factors influence perception, according to the theory, such as psychological factors like personal expectations. **[U. p4]**

4.27 **True. [M. p4]**

4.28 **True. [BX. p334]**

4.29 **False.** Most often they do not have the properties of childhood attachment. **[LL. p68]**

4.30 **True.** The term refers to the ability of an individual to display a range of characteristics from those that are traditionally held to be either masculine or feminine traits when the situation requires them. **[FF. p215]**

4.31 **False.** Dichotic listening studies show that alternative information is processed simultaneously. **[M. p7]**

4.32 **True. [BX. p418]**

4.33 **True. [LL. p109]**

4.34 **True.** Competence is a component of the needs for esteem. **[M. p12]**

4.35 **False.** When the conditioned stimulus is switched off there is an initial increase in frequency of operant behaviour before it wanes. **[QQ. p310]**

4.36 **True. [AY. p39]**

4.37 **False.** These are unrelated to attachment but are related to the socio-economic status of the family. **[LL. p104]**

4.38 **True.** The former refers to physical attraction while the latter describes a possessive type of love. **[FF. p170]**

4.39 **False.** Unless there is another cause of language delay. **[U. p33]**

4.40 **False.** It refers to the emergence of a novel behaviour without direct reinforcement of that behaviour. **[AY. p234]**

4.41 **False.** The opposite is true. **[LL. p118]**

4.42 **False.** Fear was found to produce such an effect; the response of pain was more like that produced by noradrenaline. **[FF. p145]**

4.43 **False.** This is retroactive inhibition. **[U. p8]**

4.44 **True. [BX. p419]**

4.45 **True.** Even though early secure children tend to have few friends they are trustworthy and reliable. **[LL. p105]**

4.46 **False.** Traditional models have seen it as unidirectional: a passive individual being shaped by society. **[ZZ. p40]**

4.47 **False.** It occurs as a result of institutionalisation. **[U. p68]**

4.48 **True. [AY. p506]**

4.49 **False.** Kinship bonds have a unique characteristic of sharing genes with each other. **[LL. p47]**

4.50 **True.** Men tend to pick partners who are younger and more attractive. **[ZZ. p30]**

4.51 **True.** Durkheim believed deviance made apparent the social rules of society and as a result was helpful for solidarity in society. **[FF. p326]**

4.52 **False.** Selective adaptation refers to the phenomenon whereby an individual loses some of his sensitivity to detect motion while observing motion: a result of this can be motion after-effect. **[EE. p172]**

4.53 **True. [LL. p255, 276]**

4.54 **True.** Cardinal traits are uncommon. **[BX. p419]**

4.55 **True. [M. p34]**

4.56 **True.** For example, the individual who denies his hemiplegia following a stroke. **[U. p20]**

4.57 **False.** They differ in both abilities. **[LL. p153]**

4.58 **False.** It leads to similar reduced habituation. **[I. p395]**

4.59 **True. [FF. p102]**

4.60 **True. [AY. p193]**

4.61 **True. [LL. p132]**

4.62   **False.** This is the second stage. The first and third stages are the *primal sketch* and the *object-centred representation* respectively. **[FF. p94–5]**

4.63   **False.** This is the Consolidation Theory described by Hebb. In the Encoding Deficit Theory, amnesic patients only encode the superficial characteristics of information. **[FF. p99–100]**

4.64   **False.** It is the dominant parietal lobe. **[U. p18]**

4.65   **False.** Clinging and following responses are more important than the others. **[LL. p17]**

4.66   **False.** The word can be named after the individual letters have been read. **[FF. p91]**

4.67   **True.** Although it is invariably negative. **[M. p66]**

4.68   **True.** This is the means by which a dominant group wins over a subordinated group through ideas. **[BY. p453]**

4.69   **True. [LL. p131]**

4.70   **True.** In other words, the males tended to mate with more than one female: larger body sizes are needed to compete with other males. **[ZZ. p30]**

4.71   **True.** They enjoy better physical/mental health. **[FF. p263]**

4.72   **False.** It states the opposite. **[BY. p248]**

4.73   **False.** To correct the family's own past mistakes. **[MM. p13,76]**

4.74   **True.** Correspondent inference theory has two stages: the attributions of intention and of dispositions. **[ZZ. p113]**

4.75   **False.** Myths are counter-productive. They carry the implication that family does not have to strive to solve its own problems. **[FF. p272]**

4.76   **True. [BY. p112]**

4.77   **True. [JJ. p406–9]**

4.78   **False.** Some commentators feel they are only ordinal scales (i.e. that inferences about the distances between scores are unreliable). **[ZZ. p147]**

4.79   **True. [FF. p246]**

4.80   **False.** This is the aim of radical feminism. **[BY. p379]**

4.81   **False.** Only after the subject has given responses to all the cards, does the inquiry phase of the test begin. **[JJ. p152–3]**

4.82   **False.** These two traits are part of those that contribute to the factor of *psychoticism*. **[FF. p195–6]**

4.83   **False.** It is assessed by lengthy interview, and requires extensive training. **[FF. p245]**

4.84 **True. [BY. p210]**

4.85 **True. [BD. p163]**

4.86 **False.** Epley's theory stated that seeking others' company led to a reduction of arousal. **[U. p14]**

4.87 **False.** It refers to the defensive submissive attitudes to more powerful males. **[CI. p70]**

4.88 **True. [BY. p569]**

4.89 **True.** About 40% of them will be securely attached. **[LL. p124]**

4.90 **True.** Relaxed listeners will tend to be influenced more by a communication with a high fear content. **[U. p13]**

4.91 **False.** This refers to egoistic suicide: anomie is normless (lack of regulation). **[FF. p327]**

4.92 **False.** Csikszentmihaliji's theory of flow states that both must be in balance for this attitude to occur. **[JJ. p425]**

4.93 **True. [JJ. p399]**

4.94 **False.** According to the 'triangular theory of love', romantic love is low on commitment, while consummate love is high on all three components. **[EE. p744]**

4.95 **False.** Family resilience also depends on family strengths including cohesiveness, explicit rules and pride in the family. **[FF. p227]**

4.96 **False.** The infundibulum is in the middle cranial fossa. **[BP. p694]**

4.97 **True.** As are the habenular nuclei. **[QQ. p9]**

4.98 **True.** It also sends efferent output to the putamen. **[U. p111]**

4.99 **False.** It conveys discriminative touch and proprioception. The *fasiculus gracilis* conveys vibration sense. **[QQ. p5]**

4.100 **True.** This is due to its longer course in the neck. **[BP. p873]**

4.101 **True.** It is comprised of a number of nuclei grouped into different clusters: the olfactory group, the centromedial amygdaloid group and the basolateral group. **[I. p27]**

4.102 **False.** The elements of the Papez circuit are: the hippocampus, the hypothalamus, the thalamus (anterior nucleus) and the cingulate gyrus. **[U. p115]**

4.103 **False.** It closes on day twenty-five. **[M. p94]**

4.104 **False.** They are denoted as mediodorsal, anterior and lateral. **[BQ. p184]**

4.105 **True.** This is due to involvement of corticospinal fibres descending to the spinal cord. **[BQ. p126]**

4.106 **True. [M. p217]**

4.107 **False.** Increased rCBF in Broca's area and increased perfusion of the medial prefrontal cortex have been shown. [**M. p216**]

4.108 True. [**B. p27**]

4.109 True. [**NN. p273**]

4.110 True. Those derived from pro-opiomelanocortin bind mainly to μ-receptors, while those from prodynorphin bind mainly to κ-receptors. [**QQ. p64**]

4.111 False. Neonates show very little E.E.G. activity. Infants less than one year old show desynchronised delta. [**M. p139**]

4.112 False. This would occur with a lesion in the motor area of the frontal cortex in the non-dominant hemisphere. [**AU. p378**]

4.113 False. There are only mild atrophic changes in globus pallidus. [**NN. p229**]

4.114 True. This is one of the ways this programmed cell death differs from necrosis. [**I. p34**]

4.115 False. They occur very rarely in males. [**QQ. p78**]

4.116 False. It occurs with a parietal lobe lesion. [**BR. p324**]

4.117 False. By the administration of a β-adrenergic antagonist. [**NN. p135**]

4.118 False. The former does, but inositol trisphosphate (IP_3) acts by binding to a receptor on intracellular organelles and releasing calcium from these. [**I. p78**]

4.119 False. Calcium alone is required. [**QQ. p146**]

4.120 True. They also bind Ca^{2+} ions and are involved with the breakdown of cyclic nucleotides. [**BK. p95**]

4.121 True. [**NN. p126**]

4.122 True. This peptide regulatory factor has neurotropic functions. [**A. p140**]

4.123 True. [**M. p159**]

4.124 True. This is due to the release of glucocorticoids and catecholamines. [**BK. p108**]

4.125 False. Right-handed individuals showed wider occipital lobes on the left side and wider frontal lobes on the right side. [**PP. p41**]

4.126 False. Reduced growth hormone levels are associated with depressive disorders. [**I. p110**]

4.127 True. [**M. p218**]

4.128 False. They increase delta wave activity. [**U. p144**]

4.129 True. [**NN. p213**]

4.130 False. It has a potent appetite-stimulatory action. [**AH. p237**]

4.131 True. [**QQ. p106**]

4.132 **False.** They are freely permeable. **[U. p140]**

4.133 **True.** The high affinity transport process for choline may be the rate-limiting step. **[NN. p26]**

4.134 **True.** Since serotonin-dopamine antagonists do not have this effect on the nigrostriatal area in contrast to conventional agents, this has been hypothesised to account for their reduced extra-pyramidal side-effects. **[I. p95]**

4.135 **False.** Ketanserin is a $5HT_{2C}$ antagonist. **[M. p167]**

4.136 **True.** **[BW. p57]**

4.137 **False.** They contain only two subunits. Neuromuscular receptors contain four subunits. **[B. p59]**

4.138 **True.** SRIF can affect sleep, appetite and activity in humans. **[I. p69]**

4.139 **False.** Kuhn discovered it. **[U. p153]**

4.140 **True.** As lamotrigine is enzyme inducing. **[CV. p19]**

4.141 **True.** It antagonises the AMPA and kainate subtypes of glutamate receptors. **[I. p54–7]**

4.142 **True.** While both enhance presynaptic dopamine release, the latter also releases noradrenaline. **[T. p462]**

4.143 **False.** It is an agonist at $5HT_{1A}$ receptors and an antagonist at presynaptic dopamine receptors. **[II. p133]**

4.144 **True.** If the individual is hyponatraemic; this must also be considered in individuals on carbamazepine. [Porter R, Linsley K, Ferrier N. *Treatment of severe depression – non-pharmacological aspects.* **Advances in Psychiatric Treatment** 2001; 7: 117–124.]

4.145 **True.** The mechanism is currently unknown **[I. p49]**

4.146 **True.** Pergolide may be used as adjunctive therapy for patients with Parkinson's disease treated with levodopa. **[BB. p241]**

4.147 **True.** Tachyphylaxis is the very rapid development of tolerance. **[II. p124]**

4.148 **False.** Acidification of the urine facilitates excretion. **[BK. p65]**

4.149 **True.** **[I. p2257t]**

4.150 **False.** It is somewhat shorter: 6–12 weeks as opposed to 10–12 weeks. Flupenthixol decanoate is similar to haloperidol decanoate in this regard. **[OO. p94–5]**

4.151 **False.** Paroxetine does not lower the seizure threshold. **[M. p177]**

4.152 **False.** This is a Type IV reaction. **[U. p173]**

4.153 **False.** Reduced adherence to recommended treatment. **[I. p2237]**

4.154 **False.** First-pass metabolism is marked for buspirone: less than 5%

reaches the systemic circulation. **[I. p2329]**

4.155 True. [M. p183]

4.156 False. Carbamazepine induces these hepatic isoenzymes. **[BH. p26]**

4.157 False. They selectively increase AMPA receptor (a type of glutamate receptor) gated current and improve cognitive performance. **[I. p54]**

4.158 True. There are many different modulatory sites for the $GABA_A$ receptor located in close proximity to it. **[T. p316]**

4.159 False. Increasing age gives a decreased proportion of lean mass that results in an increased volume of distribution. **[U. p163]**

4.160 False. It can reduce it. **[BL. p120]**

4.161 True. At high doses subjects are awake but dissociated from their environment. **[NN. p36]**

4.162 True. One of the differentiating facts between OCD and depression is the delay in onset of therapeutic effects in the former. **[T. p343]**

4.163 False. Cohort studies best address this. Case control/cross sectional surveys are more likely to have reverse causality. **[B. p208]**

4.164 False. It excludes the highest and lowest 2.5% of values. **[B. p165]**

4.165 True. But it needs training. **[B. p157t]**

4.166 False. It tends to rule them in: SpPin. **[SS. p121]**

4.167 True. It also gives high rates of false negatives among those with chronic psychiatric disorders. **[CF. p70]**

4.168 True. The erroneous conclusion that an intervention has no effect is more common as underpowered studies occur frequently in medical literature. **[TT. p71]**

4.169 False. This only indicates a psychiatric morbidity. **[B. p155]**

4.170 True. The median may be more appropriate than the mean for ordinal data. **[M. p229]**

4.171 False. The arcsine transformation is used for proportions; using the reciprocal is itself a transformation. **[B. p185]**

4.172 False. The preferred study design is a cross-sectional survey. **[TT. p45]**

4.173 False. So are improperly planned and improperly conducted research. **[B. p154]**

4.174 False. The χ^2 test should be used only for actual numbers, not means. **[UU. p69]**

4.175 **True. [CM. p254]**

4.176 **True. [TT. p128]**

4.177 **False.** The standard deviation is the good index of variability. **[B. p167]**

4.178 **True.** As there is an order imposed on the grades, but no inference about the difference between the grades can be made from the scale. **[RR. p5]**

4.179 **True.** An example of this is the association between blood group O and susceptibility to duodenal ulcer. **[AI. p 62]**

4.180 **False.** This is referred to as *denaturing*. **[B. p227]**

4.181 **True.** So also with another gene on the same chromosome. **[B. p222]**

4.182 **True.** Angelman syndrome is associated in some cases with uniparental disomy of this chromosome with both coming from the father. **[AI. p81]**

4.183 **False.** 0 to 0.5. This is a measure of how often alleles at two loci are separated during meiotic division. **[U. p188]**

4.184 **False.** It refers to a gene that has no obvious effect on the individual's ability to survive. **[BF. p331]**

4.185 **False.** But Cloninger type I alcoholism is. **[B. p339]**

4.186 **False.** Association studies have an important role in the study of the genetic contribution in disorders with complex transmission patterns. **[AI. p26]**

4.187 **False.** Given a certain genotype. **[AI. p46]**

4.188 **False.** It refers to the transmission of a trait exclusively through maternal relatives. **[BF. p325]**

4.189 **True.** This is the basis of the G-banding technique. **[B. p219]**

4.190 **False.** Those that arise from VNTRs usually have usually multiple alleles. **[AI. p22]**

4.191 **False.** Sperm have no mitochondria. **[B. p224]**

4.192 **True.** 1% with amniocentesis; 2–5% with chorionic villus biopsy. **[BF. p306]**

4.193 **False.** To experiencing significant life events. **[B. p412]**

4.194 **True.** It also assumes that there is no inbreeding or migration to arrive at its relation of allelic and genotypic frequencies in a given genetic population. **[AI. p39]**

4.195 **True. [B. p199]**

4.196 **False.** It is of value in such a (rare) situation. **[B. p212]**

4.197 **True. [B. p155]**

4.198 False. If it is a common exposure, this increases the PAF. **[B. p201]**

4.199 False. This is cost-utility analysis. Cost-effectiveness analysis is used when the effect of the intervention can be expressed in terms of one main variable. **[TT. p139]**

4.200 True. [C. p582]

Answers to Question Paper 5: Basic Sciences

5.1   **False.** Only the care-giving role that is directly related to the protective function is responsible for attachment having evolved. **[LL. p37]**

5.2   **False.** One of the main features of the preoperational phase is that children cannot do this. **[EE. p87]**

5.3   **True. [M. p47]**

5.4   **False.** The reverse is true. **[BX. p396]**

5.5   **True.** They show a mixture of wary and sociable behaviour. **[LL. p44]**

5.6   **True.** This refers to the child's ability to represent things by signifiers, such as mental images or language. **[I. p404]**

5.7   **False.** It occurs during the preoperational stage. **[U. p32]**

5.8   **True. [AF. p7]**

5.9   **True.** These are Youniss' (1980) and Marvin's (1977) findings. **[LL. p45–6]**

5.10 **False.** Between 5½ and 6 months of age. **[EE. p73]**

5.11 **True.** The hypothesis consists of the ideas of linguistic determinism and linguistic relativism. **[QQ. p314]**

5.12 **True. [AF. p34]**

5.13 **True.** Similarity of emotional characteristics, generalization of experience and temporal linkage all indicate this. **[LL. p69–70]**

5.14 **True.** Lack of empathy, social disinhibition, shallow relationships and developmental language delay are other effects of maternal deprivation. **[U. p27]**

5.15 **False.** It provides a measurement of social support including crisis support and individual relationships. **[FF. p245]**

5.16 **True. [AF. p9]**

5.17 **False.** This is a characteristic of A-dyad children. **[LL. p98–9]**

5.18 **True.** A previously well-learned experience interferes with processing as a result of the task being so ingrained. **[U. p6]**

5.19 **False.** It does not include institutional perspective. **[U. p78]**

5.20 **False.** It is common in older patients. **[AF. p14]**

5.21   **True.** Evolutionary theory would predict that adverse childhood experiences would augment survival and competence. **[LL. p57]**

5.22   **False.** Children up to the age of four or five show a similar pattern of response to animals. **[FF. p31–2]**

5.23   **True. [FF. p329]**

5.24   **True. [BX. p399]**

5.25   **True.** It has the most effect at retrieval. **[FF. p60]**

5.26   **False.** Wynne and colleagues proposed it in 1958. **[U. p74]**

5.27   **True. [LL. p104]**

5.28   **False.** It was developed by Lazarus. **[AF. p122]**

5.29   **True. [LL. p107]**

5.30   **False.** They react with more alarm to the object that comes closer to them, thus showing a degree of depth perception. **[G. p147]**

5.31   **True. [U. p77]**

5.32   **True.** Existence, relatedness and growth. **[CT. p376]**

5.33   **False.** Non-caring and overprotective style does. **[B. p413]**

5.34   **False.** They appear less anxious as adults. **[G. p92]**

5.35   **False.** This was Pilowsky's definition. **[M. p63]**

5.36   **True. [AU. p77]**

5.37   **False.** There is no evidence to support this. **[LL. p110]**

5.38   **False.** It is more marked in the younger children. **[ZZ. p55]**

5.39   **True. [M. p18]**

5.40   **False.** Backward conditioning is widely used. **[AU. p74]**

5.41   **True.** He has arrived at this conclusion by acknowledging that he not only thinks that he is a failure but also looks into second-order representation. **[LL. p134]**

5.42   **False.** It may be due to a common environment of individuals, although genetic transmission is likely in some cases e.g. smiling. **[ZZ. p28]**

5.43   **True.** Marcia's four statuses of identity development are: identity achievement, foreclosure, moratorium and identity diffusion. **[CR. p103]**

5.44   **False.** It is used to study unconscious motives. **[CT. p372]**

5.45   **False.** According to Ainsworth and Eichberg, both are important factors. **[LL. p46]**

5.46   **True.** In explicit memory the autobiographical components do not develop fully until after the child is two years old. **[I. p389]**

5.47   **True. [U. p18]**

5.48   **True. [AF. p36]**

5.49 **False.** Its concept is compatible with General System Theory. **[LL. p200]**

5.50 **False.** This is the cognitive ability to consider the process of thinking itself and begins about the age of six. **[I. p391]**

5.51 **True.** This is Gregory's misapplied size constancy theory. **[G. p373]**

5.52 **True. [AF. p45]**

5.53 **False.** They did not identify a uniform behaviour pattern. **[LL. p160]**

5.54 **False.** Damage to this area leads to great difficulties with both reading and writing. **[U. p19]**

5.55 **False.** The non-dominant lobe is responsible for insertion and interpretation of emotional inflexions of speech. **[M. p31]**

5.56 **True. [AF. p152]**

5.57 **False. [JJ. p445]**

5.58 **True.** It also contains the Weschler Adult Intelligence Scale. **[FF. p117]**

5.59 **False.** One less. The normal score for the former is 5±1. **[AG. p112]**

5.60 **True. [U. p21]**

5.61 **False.** It is an example of an idiographic theory. **[CU. p36–7]**

5.62 **False.** Only for those with IQs in the range: 90–128. **[AG. p204]**

5.63 **False.** Developed by H. Murray, it consists of twenty cards. The subject is instructed to make up a story about each card. **[CN. p223]**

5.64 **True. [CT. p416]**

5.65 **True.** They are personality inventories developed by Costa and McCrea. **[JJ. p212]**

5.66 **True.** Marx saw its main function was to aid the interests of the few. **[CP. p446]**

5.67 **False.** There is increased cognitive dissonance when there is little pressure to comply. **[M. p18]**

5.68 **False.** It refers to a married childless couple. **[AM. p483]**

5.69 **False.** It does not consider physiological aspects. **[NN. p340]**

5.70 **False.** This was the view of Szasz. **[CP. p430]**

5.71 **True.** Also: isolation from outside influences and no systematic procedures for considering both pros and cons of different courses of action. **[CR. p670]**

5.72 **True. [AM. p335]**

5.73   **True.** Awareness about ethnic group differences in the expression of emotions, for example, facilitates better communication. **[NN. p338–9]**

5.74   **True.** Since the term in this context does not imply opprobrium, rather it signifies individuals who act outside a culture's norms. **[CP. p219]**

5.75   **False. [M. p17]**

5.76   **True.** This refers to how the state and labour market shape women's lives. **[AM. p358]**

5.77   **True.** The core is mainly a patrilineage. **[NN. p341]**

5.78   **False.** *Exaption*: this refers to traits that served an adaptive function in the past that no longer hold this function. **[I. p488]**

5.79   **True.** They also have ego defence and social adjustment functions. **[CR. p622]**

5.80   **False.** It is the time interval between the exchanged actions that distinguishes them. **[I. p488]**

5.81   **True.** As it is unrelated to the goal of enhancing reproductive fitness. **[NN. p343]**

5.82   **False.** It holds that such strategies are not put aside, but continue to be used for the achievement of short-term goals. **[I. p487]**

5.83   **True. [U. p9]**

5.84   **False.** This is true only for the pygmy chimpanzee *(Pan paniscus)*. **[http://members.tripod.com/uakari/pan_paniscus.html]**

5.85   **True.** In Western culture it loads with happiness, but in Indonesia it loads with sadness. **[NN. p340]**

5.86   **False.** It is better understood in terms of achieving short-term goals. **[I. p485]**

5.87   **True. [G. p62]**

5.88   **True.** Ultimate causation refers to the process whereby certain traits are selected in evolution because they can confer advantage to the individual. **[I. p485]**

5.89   **False.** This is a different way of a culture shaping the expression of emotions. **[NN. p340]**

5.90   **False.** This has been termed the *cultural fallacy*. **[I. p464]**

5.91   **True.** Conrad Lorenz described this, calling it 'instinctive behaviour'. **[G. p39]**

5.92   **True.** *Etic* refers to the application of Western diagnostic categories to other cultures. **[I. p464]**

5.93   **False.** In deeper cortical layers. **[NN. p5]**

5.94 **True. [U. p115]**

5.95 **False.** The majority are corticopontine fibres. **[WW. p246]**

5.96 **True. [BQ. p42]**

5.97 **True.** It follows the striosome (low density) – matrix (high density) organisation. **[NN. p17]**

5.98 **True.** It is part of the superior raphe nuclei system. **[U. p123]**

5.99 **False.** All except the hippocampus, which is part of the telencephalon. **[M. p94]**

5.100 **True.** It herniates through the tentorial incisure and causes kinking of the occulomotor nerve. **[BP. p698]**

5.101 **True.** This is due to pressure on the optic chiasma. **[BP. p687]**

5.102 **True.** It is also called the island of Reil. **[QQ. p18]**

5.103 **True. [M. p120]**

5.104 **True.** The optic atrophy is caused by compression of the optic nerve and papilloedema by the secondary raised intra-cranial pressure. **[BR. p322]**

5.105 **True. [PP. p548]**

5.106 **False.** They increase in size as well. **[AH. p187]**

5.107 **False.** It tends to be fairly rapid in its progression. **[AH. p189]**

5.108 **True.** This refers to the progressively increasing group response of neurons to a repetitive stimulus of uniform strength. **[BQ. p225]**

5.109 **False.** Memory disturbances can, at times, reach the level of Korsakoff's syndrome. **[PP. p636]**

5.110 **True.** This response is blunted in at least 25% of depressed individuals. **[QQ. p75–6]**

5.111 **True.** The expectancy wave is another name for the *contingent negative variation*. **[M. p142]**

5.112 **True. [B. p32]**

5.113 **False.** Vacuolar myelopathy is a distinctive finding confined to the spinal cord. **[PP. p323]**

5.114 **False.** The lateral zone is the hunger centre, while the medial zone is the satiety centre. **[QQ. p58]**

5.115 **True. [M. p135]**

5.116 **False.** The opposite is true. **[BN. p90]**

5.117 **False.** Ukhtomski has shown that in a dog learned motor behaviour was non-localised. **[NN. p329]**

5.118 **False.** Renshaw cells are located in the anterior horn. They produce an inhibitory negative feedback to alpha motor neurones. **[QQ. p42]**

5.119 False. Some G proteins act by inhibiting adenyl cyclase. **[AH. p227]**

5.120 True. [BN. p190]

5.121 False. If it was preceded by two weeks. **[NN. p107]**

5.122 True. Dopamine and opioids also stimulate its release while somatostatin reduces its release. **[AH. p240]**

5.123 True. [U. p151]

5.124 False. Into the metencephalon and the myelencephalon. **[U. p107]**

5.125 True. [NN. p265]

5.126 True. Its receptor is similar to that of insulin also. **[AH. p232]**

5.127 False. CHAT activity is inhibited by acetylcholine (product inhibition). **[M. p150]**

5.128 True. This may reflect a change in dopamine activity. **[BN. p73]**

5.129 True. [I. p57]

5.130 False. Only the following are linked to the phosphotidylinositol system: $5HT_{2A}$, $5HT_{2B}$, $5HT_{2C}$. **[M. p166]**

5.131 False. It is found throughout most of the CNS, but especially in the hypothalamus, limbic system and cerebral cortex. **[U. p152]**

5.132 False. They lie in the diencephalon. **[B. p34]**

5.133 False. If properly controlled, TMS can demonstrate this. **[B. p461]**

5.134 True. Also with the severity of depression in patients with multiple sclerosis and Huntington disease. **[I. p68]**

5.135 True. Also by competitive inhibition at the tyrosine binding site. **[M. p153]**

5.136 False. [CB. p197]

5.137 False. They are not subtypes but subunits of the NMDA receptor. **[I. p55]**

5.138 False. It has a roughly similar duration of action but a much slower onset of action. **[T. p328–31]**

5.139 False. Risperidone does not cause agranulocytosis. **[M. p174]**

5.140 True. They enhance serotonergic neurotransmission. **[BL. p129]**

5.141 True. [I. p176]

5.142 False. This is associated with topiramate. **[T. p271]**

5.143 True. [U. p177]

5.144 True. [BI. p108]

5.145 False. In patients with symmetry obsessions. **[I. p1496]**

5.146 False. While no time during pregnancy is particularly safe, the greatest risk period is roughly from 17 to 60 days post-conception.

[AB. p80]

5.147 **False.** 3–5%. **[M. p174]**

5.148 **True.** In addition to the hepatic microsomal system. **[BN. p55]**

5.149 **True.** One study reported 92% of heroin abusers using temazepam. **[NN. p877]**

5.150 **False.** While donepezil undergoes glucuronidation, rivastigmine is not metabolised by the liver. **[I. p2349–51]**

5.151 **True.** **[II. p28]**

5.152 **False.** Ethanol decreases the plasma levels of these drugs through enzyme induction. **[BN. p135]**

5.153 **True.** Levonantradol and nabilone are synthetic cannabinoids and they have been used in patients with AIDS and cancer patients to control G.I. symptoms. **[NN. p816]**

5.154 **True.** Since plasma levels of free drug are increased. **[OO. p247]**

5.155 **False.** Phase II involves synthetic reactions. **[M. p192]**

5.156 **True.** **[B. p112]**

5.157 **False.** They block long-term maintenance, whereas protein kinase inhibitors inhibit the initiation of LTP. **[NN. p63]**

5.158 **True.** The text cited quotes Ray *et al.* (1989). **[L. p124]**

5.159 **False.** Ataxia is a sign of the toxic effects of lithium overdose. **[M. p180]**

5.160 **True.** **[B. p120]**

5.161 **False.** Twin studies did not support this. **[B. p342]**

5.162 **False.** Irregularities in classical transmission could be explained by incomplete penetrance or variable expression. **[AI. p45–6]**

5.163 **False.** Semi-discontinuous. **[M. p193]**

5.164 **True.** It stipulates: a large population, no migration, random mating and a constant rate of mutation. **[BF. p243]**

5.165 **False.** **[B. p221]**

5.166 **True.** This refers to differing expression of gene(s) depending on whether inheritance comes from the mother or the father. In Huntington's disease, early onset of symptoms is associated with parental transmission. **[AI. p14]**

5.167 **True.** **[AI. p33]**

5.168 **False.** It is a term used in segregation analysis. **[BF. p329]**

5.169 **True.** But this is an expensive method. **[B. p230]**

5.170 **False.** There have been replicated positive associations described for HLA A9 and B5 and one negative one for BW35. **[AI. p100]**

5.171 **True.** [Muir WJ. *Genetics advances and learning disability*. **British**

Journal of Psychiatry 2000; 176: 12–18.]

5.172 True. Along with somatic mutations and repeat sequence expansions. **[B. p226]**

5.173 True. [B. p380]

5.174 False. Between 50,000 and 100,000 genes is generally quoted in the texts, although recent findings indicate there may be as few as 35,000. **[I. p172]**

5.175 False. Autosomal recessive disorders tend to display horizontal transmission. **[QQ. p179]**

5.176 True. The LOD score is a mathematical measure of the likelihood of linkage. **[BF. p107]**

5.177 False. This refers to sensitivity. **[B. p156]**

5.178 False. Adults living in institutions were also assessed. **[I. p518]**

5.179 True. Interviewers without a clinical background can use it. **[B. p158]**

5.180 False. This refers to a screening procedure. **[C. p1265]**

5.181 False. Not statistically significant, rather clinically significant. **[TT. p63]**

5.182 False. It also has relatively poor reliability for diagnosing alcoholism. **[QQ. p307]**

5.183 True. [B. p199]

5.184 False. In this case a cost-effectiveness analysis would be appropriate. **[TT. p153]**

5.185 True. [B. p169]

5.186 True. The inception rate is the number of individuals per defined population who develop the disease in the given interval, having been free of the illness originally. **[A. p214]**

5.187 False. Cronbach alpha scores of 0.90 are required for individual screening. Score of 0.70–0.80 are required for group comparison. **[CN. p33]**

5.188 True. [BE. p233]

5.189 False. [B. p166]

5.190 True. Chronicity refers to how long the given disease tends to last. **[QQ. p304]**

5.191 True. Natural units include 'months of survival'. **[TT. p144]**

5.192 False. Treatment periods are replicated until the clinician and patient are convinced that the treatments are definitely different or definitely not different. **[BE. p247]**

5.193 False. This is the probability of the outcome not occurring $(1 - P)$.

[B. p163]

5.194 **False.** This is the *accuracy* of the test. **[TT. p101]**

5.195 **True.** Using the product moment correlation there is more likely to be a chance agreement than with the kappa. **[QQ. p289]**

5.196 **True. [C. p1265]**

5.197 **True. [B. p173]**

5.198 **True.** NNT = 1/(CER – EER). **[SS. p135]**

5.199 **False.** 0.99 inter rater reliability. 0.93 test retest reliability. [Reynolds T, Thornicroft G, Abas M, *et al. Camberwell Assessment of Need for the Elderly (CANE): Development, validity and reliability.* **British Journal of Psychiatry** 2000; 176: 444–452.]

5.200 **True.** Also known as the pre-test prevalence. **[http://cebmh.com]**

Answers to Question Paper 6: Basic Sciences

6.1   **False.** Securely attached B-dyads tend to communicate in this way. **[LL. p98]**

6.2   **True.** Once one navigates past the double negative, one is left with the simple fact that infants prefer contrasting patterns to plain ones. **[EE. p80]**

6.3   **False.** The phoneme is the essential unit: the morpheme is the meaningful unit of sound. **[M. p52]**

6.4   **True. [AF. p31]**

6.5   **False.** Unlike some of the insecurely attached children, the majority of the securely attached stated this. **[LL. p103]**

6.6   **True.** This is probably the case since the individual is required to reflect on his/her own thinking processes. **[I. p412]**

6.7   **True. [M. p47]**

6.8   **False.** The opposite is true. **[AF. p32]**

6.9   **True. [LL. p120–1]**

6.10 **False.** This has been shown for the family structures of single parents or large family size, but not for the extended family or two lesbian parent structures. **[U. p28]**

6.11 **False.** This is the age for the realisation of conservation of quantity, however the concept of conservation of weight usually develops about the age of 9–10. **[I. p405]**

6.12 **False.** This is the case with top-down processing in recognition. **[AF. p22]**

6.13 **False.** They view that both are conceptually distinct and therefore incompatible. **[LL. p136]**

6.14 **True.** A diminished sense of gender identity is also associated with child sexual abuse. **[U. p29]**

6.15 **True. [U. p69]**

6.16 **False.** Its founder was William James. **[BX. p10]**

6.17 **False.** 8 out of 9 patients studied by Parkes described a significant association to parental influences. **[LL. p276]**

6.18 **True.** An increased anxiolytic effect can also be produced from the same mechanism. **[FF. p25]**

6.19 **False.** This is avoidance conditioning. **[M. p3]**

6.20 **False.** He described a series of stages in the dying process. **[AF. p16]**

6.21 **False.** An attachment has all the qualities of affect ional bonds. **[LL. p38]**

6.22 **False.** A *knowledge* function. **[EE. p729–30]**

6.23 **True.** It is a psychodynamic theory covering aspects of prejudice. **[G. p227]**

6.24 **False.** These would be at the subordinate level. **[CT. p415]**

6.25 **True. [LL. p132]**

6.26 **True.** The same apples for neuroticism scores. **[FF. p171]**

6.27 **False.** Aversive conditioning includes punishment, avoidance and escape conditioning. **[M. p3]**

6.28 **True. [AU. p88]**

6.29 **False.** A recent review has emphasised the role of cognitive factors. **[LL. p138–9]**

6.30 **False.** They do, but it typically takes longer to develop: usually about 15 months. **[EE. p497]**

6.31 **True. [FF. p26]**

6.32 **False.** It is one of the components of working memory. **[AU. p81]**

6.33 **False.** The film was about attachment and consequences of temporary separation from the child's mother. **[LL. p15]**

6.34 **True.** According to Tompkins (1962). **[EE. p433]**

6.35 **False.** This is his Specificity Principle. The Systems Principle states that emotion is a complex and ever changing phenomenon. **[FF. p141]**

6.36 **False.** It is recollection of past experiences based on certain cues. **[AU. p82]**

6.37 **True.** But it could be modified appropriately for each culture. **[LL. p59–60]**

6.38 **False.** Like humans, chimpanzees make few irrelevant moves once they have solved the puzzle. **[EE. p281]**

6.39 **False.** They tend to under-use it, especially *explicit consensus*, which refers to how a group of individuals will behave, as opposed to the observer's beliefs about how they would behave (*implicit consensus*). **[ZZ. p130]**

6.40 **False.** The former is one which is known only to the sufferer and a few close intimates while the latter is obvious to the world at large. **[AF. p121]**

6.41 **True. [JJ. p400]**

6.42 **True.** These are individuals who are obedient to those they see as their superiors but contemptuous towards those they see as inferior. **[EE. p731]**

6.43 **True. [U. p70]**

6.44 **False.** They refer to aspects of verbal messages that serve to modulate their meaning. **[AF. p92]**

6.45 **True. [JJ. p115]**

6.46 **False.** Presentation of cues involves peripheral pathways. Central pathways involve the consideration of new information. **[U. p13]**

6.47 **True.** Their reaction times tend to be slower if the given stimuli were of differing modalities: the modality shift effect. **[I. p394]**

6.48 **False.** This is rarely associated with elation in organic conditions. **[Q. p73]**

6.49 **False. [BD. p21]**

6.50 **True.** The lexical route enables words with irregular sounds for their spellings to be read correctly. **[FF. p88–9]**

6.51 **True. [M. p29]**

6.52 **False.** They may present with either one of these difficulties. **[BD. p160]**

6.53 **False.** The opposite is true. Some consider this as a third form of alexia. **[BD. p169]**

6.54 **True.** While this does not always occur, it is hypothesized to result from either learned coping mechanisms or neuronal sprouting. **[W. p543]**

6.55 **True.** They are called 'peripheral dyslexias' because they are hypothesised as deriving from less central parts of the reading system. **[FF. p91]**

6.56 **False.** Anterior temporal lobectomy causes this effect. **[BD. p209–10]**

6.57 **False.** Often it is revealed only on neuropsychological examination. **[BD. p261]**

6.58 **True.** It was first described by Freud and refers to a child's earliest memories beginning at approximately three years of age. **[CR. p288]**

6.59 **False.** Since the NMDA receptor is initially blocked by Mg^{2+} ions, glutamate has to bind first to non-NMDA receptors causing depolarisation, which temporarily removes the Mg^{2+} ions. **[W. p478–9]**

6.60 True. [BD. p213–4]

6.61 True. It causes tonal loss in both ears and digits defects in the left ear. [BD. p208]

6.62 True. Perceptual defence is the phenomenon whereby most people take longer to identify sexual or obscene words. Others (perceptual sensitisation) identify these words more easily than neutral words. [G. p365]

6.63 False. It may also result from frontal lobe lesions. [AG. p69]

6.64 True. [BD. p265t]

6.65 True. [BD. p185]

6.66 True. They have difficulties in recalling colours of objects when asked. [AG. p88]

6.67 True. But the patterns of difficulties in producing the figure differ and may aid localisation of lesions. [AG. p211–2]

6.68 False. This describes pseudowords. [AY. p321]

6.69 True. Dismissing parents are excessively succinct. [LL. p143–4]

6.70 False. Barton (1959) used this term. [QQ. p333–4]

6.71 True. [G. p227]

6.72 False. He considered that society was in constant change and struggle and that revolution was inevitable. [CP. p535]

6.73 True. This is because of the caretaker's consistently refusing to listen to the child's statements during its preschool years. [LL. p219–22]

6.74 False. Since such a team does not operate on bureaucratic rules. [FF. p336]

6.75 True. He thought that language has its own separate genetic routes in an innate language acquisition device. [FF. p75]

6.76 False. This reflects ethnographers' claims that one should not make false distinction between thought and feeling. [NN. p339]

6.77 True. [LL. p220]

6.78 True. Since the explicit rules of conduct ensure patient care and organisation are performed. [FF. p335]

6.79 False. Studies show that, with practice, digit spans can be increased; also some people possess an innate superior faculty. [FF. p59]

6.80 False. It is stored in the right hemisphere and is recalled effortlessly and error-free. [M. p9]

6.81 True. In their longitudinal study, Peterson and Mehl reported this finding. [LL. p40]

6.82 **True.** There is a fifth outcome, considered non-deviant: conformity. **[FF. p328]**

6.83 **False.** While Chomsky and Greenberg were nativists, Skinner was a behaviourist. **[G. p159]**

6.84 **True. [NN. p341]**

6.85 **False.** Evolutionary process views sociopathy as an adaptation to increase reproductive success. **[NN. p344]**

6.86 **False.** He felt that all forms of deviance helped social integration in that individuals would unite in their abhorrence of it. **[FF. p326–7]**

6.87 **True.** It uses a database system for scoring and interpreting the Rorschach. **[CN. p23]**

6.88 **False.** On both. **[NN. p340]**

6.89 **False.** Bowlby used this to describe the hunting-and-gathering way of life. **[NN. p342]**

6.90 **True.** This is the practice of choosing a marriage partner within the same ethnic group. **[FF. p302]**

6.91 **True. [NN. p401]**

6.92 **False.** This psychological mechanism is similar to pheromones preventing incest in other species. **[NN. p348]**

6.93 **True.** They do feel depression but expresses it somatically. **[NN. p340]**

6.94 **False.** The pygmy chimpanzee *(Pan paniscus)* uses such activity as a part of social communication. **[http://members.tripod.com/ uakari/pan_paniscus.html]**

6.95 **True.** Impulses involved in these reflexes probably come from proprioceptive receptors or the vestibular apparatus. **[WW. p249]**

6.96 **False.** These lesions are associated with apathy and hypokinesia. **[BQ. p205]**

6.97 **True.** While the third ventricle connects to the fourth via the cerebral aqueduct. **[I. p9]**

6.98 **False.** The globus pallidus and the putamen. **[QQ. p7]**

6.99 **True.** It is involved in autonomic function and in taste. **[M. p100]**

6.100 **False.** The pulvinar is situated in the dorsal portion of the thalamus. **[I. p12]**

6.101 **False.** There are three: the hippocampus, the dentate gyrus and the subiculum. **[I. p26]**

6.102 **False.** It lies on the superior surface of the corpus callosum. **[QQ. p24]**

6.103 **True. [U. p131]**

6.104 **False.** The lateral nucleus in the tuberal region is associated with this. **[NN. p23]**

6.105 **True.** As they are involved in the Papez circuit. **[NN. p19]**

6.106 **True.** They tend to cause a motor peripheral neuropathy. Organic forms can cause encephalopathy in adults. **[AH. p208]**

6.107 **False.** Increased phospomonoesterases have been shown. **[M. p217]**

6.108 **True.** It is associated with dopaminergic neuronal degeneration in the pars compacta. **[I. p18]**

6.109 **False.** The reverse is true although the relevance is not clear. **[BK. p61]**

6.110 **False.** It develops from the neural plate, which is of ectodermal origin. **[I. p32]**

6.111 **False.** It is a graded response with no refractory period and does summate. **[M. p148]**

6.112 **True.** **[I. p49]**

6.113 **False.** The ion must be negative to cause this effect. **[BO. p82]**

6.114 **True.** **[QQ. p80]**

6.115 **True.** While that of K^+ is $-96\,mV$. **[I. p85]**

6.116 **False.** It is not involved in synaptic signalling. **[I. p52]**

6.117 **True.** The centre concerned is proposed to lie in the posterior hypothalamus. **[BK. p59]**

6.118 **True.** Late long-term potentiation processes that involve activation of protein kinases can be affected since D_1 and D_5 receptors cause increased cAMP when activated. **[I. p39]**

6.119 **False.** It is normal. **[M. p223]**

6.120 **True.** It also has control over various autonomic functions. **[AH. p235]**

6.121 **True.** **[I. p49]**

6.122 **True.** Galanin has a number of actions of clinical interest such as inhibition of noradrenaline firing in the locus ceruleus and acetylcholine release as well as memory impairment. **[I. p107]**

6.123 **False.** This theory is the transmethylation theory of schizophrenia. **[QQ. p126]**

6.124 **True.** **[CB. p293]**

6.125 **True.** **[NN. p111]**

6.126 **False.** Only the $G_{s\alpha}$ subunit is bound to GDP; the $G_{s\beta}$ and the $G_{s\gamma}$ subunits are bound to the cell membrane. **[AH. p227]**

6.127 **True.** Its injection into the third ventricle antagonises the satiety action of exogenous cholecystokinin-8. **[QQ. p61]**

6.128 True. Malloy found in almost two-thirds of cases evidence of brain damage. **[PP. p15]**

6.129 False. This is the function of luteinizing hormone. **[BU. p304]**

6.130 False. It is a precursor of GABA, but it acts as an excitatory neurotransmitter. **[I. p51]**

6.131 True. D1-like receptors are linked via Gs to adenylate cyclase. **[M. p165]**

6.132 True. [I. p58]

6.133 True. [B. p35]

6.134 True. Polymorphisms of the tryptophan hydroxylase gene have been associated with suicidal behaviour. **[QQ. p127]**

6.135 False. Increased cholinergic activity. **[QQ. p117]**

6.136 False. Both have been found to be decreased in such individuals. **[I. p107]**

6.137 True. The COMT pathway produces VMA alone, while the MAO pathway has two main routes producing VMA or MHPG. **[U. p150]**

6.138 False. This worsening of symptomatology does not happen, unlike in depression. **[T. p343–4]**

6.139 True. [U. p164]

6.140 False. The drug is 50% ionised in this situation. **[BK. p131]**

6.141 False. Caffeine blocks adenosine receptors. **[I. p984]**

6.142 True. If a drug must be given to a breast-feeding mother it is usually best to try to give it as a single dose before the baby's longest sleep period and breast-feed the baby just before this dose. **[AB. p86]**

6.143 False. It is curvilinear. **[II. p39]**

6.144 True. And vice-versa. **[BK. p139]**

6.145 False. Pharmacotherapy is not useful in controlling paruresis. **[I. p1497]**

6.146 False. Valproate is contraindicated in severe liver disease: lithium and gabapentin are the mood stabilisers of choice. **[AB. p93–4]**

6.147 False. This is a phase I trial. Phase II trials involve clinical efficacy and further clinical pharmacology. **[II. p49]**

6.148 True. Pre-synaptic elimination refers to first-pass metabolism. **[BK. p136]**

6.149 True. [I. p2257t]

6.150 False. Within two hours. **[I. p2390]**

6.151 **True.** [**T. p271**]

6.152 **False.** The former is twice the latter. [**BK. p141**]

6.153 **True.** [**NN. p51**]

6.154 **True.** Most studies however suggest that mirtazepine is better tolerated. [**I. p2392–3**]

6.155 **True.** Metaraminol is an alpha agonist. [**II. p461**]

6.156 **False.** Peak levels are attained in 30–60 minutes. [**B. p128**]

6.157 **True.** It remains morally justifiable if only a reasonable possibility exists. [**B. p155**]

6.158 **False.** Thioridazine has been most associated with this. [**I. p2372**]

6.159 **False.** It is not as effective in blocking the emotional aspects of anxiety. [**T. p307**]

6.160 **True.** [**C. p389**]

6.161 **True.** [**U. p158**]

6.162 **False.** This can differ by up to 60%. [**I. p2251**]

6.163 **False.** This is a reciprocal translocation. A Robertsonian translocation is fusion of two chromosomes at the centromere. [**AI. p7**]

6.164 **True.** Both may serve as genetic markers. [**I. p179**]

6.165 **False.** The *Taq-1* polymorphism association reported by a number of studies was in the dopamine D_2 receptor gene. [**AI. p170**]

6.166 **True.** [**B. p229**]

6.167 **False.** Autosomal dominant. [**U. p189**]

6.168 **True.** This is because in the former some twins will be counted twice if they have been independently ascertained. [**B. p226**]

6.169 **False.** This is linkage disequilibrium. [**I. p177**]

6.170 **True.** Since the former reduces the number of patients one can identify and thus reduces the power of the study. [**I. p185**]

6.171 **False.** X-linked dominant. [**U. p191**]

6.172 **False.** Epistasis is the interaction of genes; fragile X syndrome is thought to result from a trinucleotide repeat sequence in a single major gene. [**I. p174–6**]

6.173 **True.** A LOD score of 3.3 or higher implies significance ($p < 0.05$). [**I. p182**]

6.174 **True.** As is fragile X syndrome. [**I. p174**]

6.175 **False.** A trio refers to the affected patient and his two parents. [**I. p178**]

6.176 **True.** Since it is measured on a continuous scale. This contrasts to qualitative phenotypes such as disease status. [**I. p174**]

6.177 **False.** [**B. p162**]

6.178 False. 'One-way' ANOVA deals with only one independent variable. **[RR. p299–300]**

6.179 False. It is designed mainly to measure symptomatology in schizophrenia, especially catatonic symptoms. **[A. p178]**

6.180 True. It is calculated by the formula: (1 – sensitivity)/specificity. **[http://cebm.jr2.ox.ac.uk/docs/likerats.html]**

6.181 True. Rating scales are used for this purpose. **[B. p159]**

6.182 False. It is an example of a discrete probability distribution. **[M. p228]**

6.183 True. As expected trait anxiety correlates with other anxiety measures. **[CF. p76]**

6.184 True. This is one school of thought. **[B. p162]**

6.185 False. It has an unstable analytical structure. **[B. p160]**

6.186 True. While both provide less high quality evidence than randomised controlled trials, they may be the only appropriate designs for particular studies. **[TT. p47]**

6.187 True. [CN. p34]

6.188 False. Fifteen psychiatric disorders. **[B. p157]**

6.189 True. [B. p170]

6.190 True. The Mann-Whitney U test is used for unpaired data. **[UU. p93]**

6.191 True. [B. p158]

6.192 False. This is an advantage of case-control studies. **[BJ. p72]**

6.193 True. [B. p201]

6.194 False. Procedural validity looks at whether a specified group of users of the instrument can use it and get the same results as those who are skilled in its use. **[I. p506]**

6.195 False. From conception to the time of onset. **[BJ. p64]**

6.196 True. Plausibility refers to one being able to put forward a theory of causation based on known facts of the disease: such knowledge may be lacking in newly described illnesses. **[I. p510]**

6.197 False. A nested case-control study is conducted by following up those patients that develop the illness in the setting of a cohort study that is running. **[CQ. p57]**

6.198 False. They used the Diagnostic Interview Schedule. **[I. p517–8]**

6.199 True. The trauma is necessary, but not all experiencing a trauma will develop the disorder. **[BJ. p60–1]**

6.200 False. Overmatching means that there is matching on the exposure variable as well, thus reducing power. **[CQ. p55]**

References Texts

Note: References in the answer section are given in the format: [F. p294]. This indicates that the topic relating to that particular MCQ may be found on page 294 of the text listed at 'F' below.

A. Kendell RE, Zealley AK, editors. *Companion to Psychiatric Studies.* 5th edn. London: Churchill Livingstone, 1993.

B. Johnstone EC, Freeman CPL, Zealley AK, editors. *Companion to Psychiatric Studies.* 6th edn. London: Churchill Livingstone, 1998.

C. Stein G, Wilkinson G, editors. *Seminars in General Adult Psychiatry.* London: Gaskell, 1998.

D. Healy D. *The Anti-depressant Era.* Cambridge (MA): Harvard University Press, 1997.

E. Kaplan HI, Sadock BJ. *Pocket Handbook of Psychiatric Drug Treatment.* Baltimore (MD): Williams & Wilkins, 1993.

F. Kaplan HI, Sadock BJ. *Pocket Handbook of Clinical Psychiatry.* Baltimore (MD): Williams & Wilkins, 1990.

G. Eysenck M. *Simply Psychology.* Hove: Psychology Press, 1996.

H. Sims A. *Symptoms in the Mind: an Introduction to Descriptive Psychopathology.* 2nd edn. London: W. B. Saunders Company Ltd., 1995.

I. Sadock BJ, Sadock VA, editors. *Kaplan & Sadock's Comprehensive Textbook of Psychiatry.* 7th edn. Philadelphia (PA): Lippincott Williams & Wilkins, 2000.

J. Brown D, Pedder J. *Introduction to Psychotherapy: an Outline of Psychodynamic Principles and Practice.* 2nd edn. London: Routledge, 1991.

K. Bateman A, Holmes J. *Introduction to Psychoanalysis: Contemporary Theory and Practice.* London: Routledge, 1995.

L. Marneros A, editor. *Late-Onset Mental Disorders: the Potsdam Conference.* London: Gaskell, 1999.

M. Malhi, GS, Mitchell AJ. *Examination Notes in Psychiatry, Basic Sciences: a Postgraduate Text.* Oxford: Butterworth-Heinemann, 1999.

N. Butler R, Pitt B, editors. *Seminars in Old Age Psychiatry.* London:

Gaskell, 1998.

O. Hawton K, Salkovskis PM, Kirk J, Clark DM, editors. *Cognitive Behaviour Therapy for Psychiatric Problems: a Practical Guide.* Oxford: Oxford University Press, 1989.

P. Goodman R, Scott S. *Child Psychiatry.* Oxford: Blackwell Science, 1997.

Q. Hamilton M, editor. *Fish's Clinical Psychopathology: Signs and Symptoms in Psychiatry.* Revised reprint. Bristol: John Wright & Sons Ltd., 1974.

R. Puri BK, Sklar J. *Examination Notes for the MRCPsych Part I.* Kent: Butterworths, 1989.

S. Stahl SM. *Psychopharmacology of Antipsychotics.* London: Martin Dunitz, 1999.

T. Stahl SM. *Essential Psychopharmacology: Neuroscientific Basis and Practical Applications.* 2nd edn. Cambridge: Cambridge University Press, 2000.

U. Puri BK, Hall AD. *Revision Notes in Psychiatry.* London: Arnold, 1998.

V. Buckley P, Bird J, Harrison G. *Examination Notes in Psychiatry: A Postgraduate Text.* 3rd edn. Oxford: Butterworth-Heinemann, 1995.

W. Kalat JW. *Biological Psychology.* 5th edn. Pacific Grove (CA): Brooks/Cole, 1995.

X. Gelder G, Gath D, Mayou R, Cowen P. *Oxford Textbook of Psychiatry.* 3rd edn. Oxford: Oxford University Press, 1996.

Y. Stahl SM. *Psychopharmacology of Antidepressants.* London: Martin Dunitz, 1999.

Z. Silverstone T, Turner P. *Drug Treatment in Psychiatry.* 5th edn. London: Routledge, 1995.

AA. Hughes P. *Dynamic Psychotherapy Explained.* Oxford: Radcliffe Medical Press, 1999.

BB. British Medical Association and the Royal Pharmaceutical Society of Great Britain. *British National Formulary.* Number 42. London: The Pharmaceutical Press, 2001.

CC. Jacob LS. *Pharmacology: the National Medical Series for Independent Study.* Baltimore (MD): Williams & Wilkins, 1992.

DD. McKenna PJ. *Schizophrenia and Related Syndromes.* Hove: Psychology Press, 1997.

EE. Atkinson RL, Atkinson RC, Smith EE, Bem DJ. *Introduction to Psychology.* 11th edn. Orlando (FL): Harcourt Brace, 1993.

FF. Tantam D, Birchwood M, editors. *Seminars in Psychology and the Social*

Sciences. London: Gaskell, 1994.

GG. World Health Organization. *The ICD-10 Classification of Mental and Behavioural Disorders: Clinical Descriptions and Diagnostic Guidelines.* Geneva: World Health Organization, 1992.

HH. American Psychiatric Association. *Diagnostic and Statistical Manual of Mental Disorders Fourth Edition: DSM-IV.* Washington (DC): American Psychiatric Association, 1994.

II. King DJ. *Seminars in Clinical Psychopharmacology.* London: Gaskell, 1995.

JJ. Liebert RM, Liebert LL. *Liebert & Spiegler's Personality Strategies and Issues.* 8th edn. Pacific Grove (CA): Brooks/Cole, 1998.

KK. Clark DM, Fairburn CG, editors. *Science and Practice of Cognitive Behaviour Therapy.* Oxford: Oxford University Press, 1997.

LL. Parkes CM, Stevenson-Hinde J, Marris P, editors. *Attachment Across the Life Cycle.* London: Routledge, 1991.

MM. Bloch S, Hafner J, Harari E, Szmukler GI. *The Family in Clinical Psychiatry.* Oxford: Oxford University Press, 1994.

NN. Kaplan HI, Sadock BJ, editors. *Comprehensive Textbook of Psychiatry.* 6th edn. Baltimore (MD): Williams & Wilkins, 1995.

OO. Bazire S. *Psychotropic Drug Directory 1998: the Professionals' Pocket Handbook & Aide Memoire.* Salisbury: Quay Books, 1998.

PP. Lishman WA. *Organic Psychiatry.* 3rd edn. Oxford: Blackwell Science, 1998.

QQ. Puri BK, Tyrer PJ. *Sciences Basic to Psychiatry.* 2nd edn. Edinburgh: Churchill Livingstone, 1998.

RR. Howell DC. *Statistical Methods for Psychology.* 4th edn. Belmont (CA): Duxbury Press, 1997.

SS. Sackett DL, Richardson WS, Rosenberg W, Haynes RB. *Evidence-based Medicine: How to Practice & Teach EBM.* Edinburgh: Churchill Livingstone, 1998.

TT. Greenhalgh T. *How to Read a Paper: The Basics of Evidence Based Medicine.* London: BMJ Publishing Group, 1997.

UU. Swinscow TDV. *Statistics at Square One.* 9th edn. London: BMJ Publishing Group, 1996.

VV. Gelder MG, López-Ibor JJ, Andreasen N, editors. *New Oxford Textbook of Psychiatry.* Oxford: Oxford University Press, 2000.

WW. Romanes GJ. *Cunningham's Manual of Practical Anatomy Volume Three: Head and Neck and Brain.* Oxford: Oxford Medical Publications, 1989.

XX. Chiswick D, Cope R, editors. *Seminars in Practical Forensic Psychiatry.*

London: Gaskell, 1995.

YY. Russell O. *Seminars in the Psychiatry of Learning Disabilities.* London: Gaskell, 1997.

ZZ. Hewstone M, Stroebe W, Codol JP, Stephenson GM, editors. *Introduction to Social Psychology: a European Perspective.* Oxford: Blackwell, 1998.

AB. Taylor D, McConnell D, McConnell H, Abel K, Kerwin R. *The Bethlem & Maudsley NHS Trust 1999 Prescribing Guidelines.* 5th edn. London: Martin Dunitz, 1999.

AC. Black D, Cottrell D, editors. *Seminars in Child and Adolescent Psychiatry.* London: Gaskell, 1993.

AD. Chick J, Cantwell R, editors. *Seminars in Alcohol and Drug Misuse.* London: Gaskell, 1994.

AE. Jacoby R, Oppenheimer C, editors. *Psychiatry in the Elderly.* 2nd edn. Oxford: Oxford University Press, 1997.

AF. Porter M, Alder B, Abraham C. *Psychology and Sociology Applied to Medicine.* London: Churchill Livingstone, 2000.

AG. Hodges JR. *Cognitive Assessments for Clinicians.* Oxford: Oxford University Press, 1994.

AH. Morgan G, Butler S, editors. *Seminars in Basic Neurosciences.* London: Gaskell, 1993.

AI. McGuffin P, Owen MJ, O'Donovan MC, Thapar A, Gottesman II. *Seminars in Psychiatric Genetics.* London: Gaskell, 1994.

AJ. Osborne R. *Freud for Beginners.* New York: Writers and Readers, 1993.

AK. Lee A, editor. *Acute Psychosis, Schizophrenia and Comorbid Disorders: Recent Topics from Advances in Psychiatric Treatment.* Vol.1. London: Gaskell, 1998.

AL. Shorter E. *A History of Psychiatry: From the Era of the Asylum to the Age of Prozac.* New York: John Wiley & Sons Inc., 1997.

AM. Enoch D, Trethowan W. *Uncommon Psychiatric Syndromes.* 3rd edn. Oxford: Butterworth-Heinemann, 1991.

AN. Casey P, Craven C. *Psychiatry and the Law.* Dublin: Oak Tree Press, 1999.

AO. Frangou S, Murray RM. *Schizophrenia.* 2nd edn. London: Martin Dunitz, 2000.

AP. Guthrie E, Creed F, editors. *Seminars in Liaison Psychiatry.* London: Gaskell, 1996.

AQ. Knight B. *Legal Aspects of Medical Practice.* 5th edn. London: Churchill

Livingstone, 1992.

AR. Robertson MM, Katona CLE, editors. *Perspectives in Psychiatry*, Vol. 6: *Depression and Physical Illness*. Chichester: John Wiley & Sons Ltd, 1997.

AS. Platania J. *Jung for Beginners*. London: Writers and Readers Book, 1997.

AT. Goldberg D, editor. *The Maudsley Handbook of Practical Psychiatry*. Oxford: Oxford Medical Publications, 1997.

AU. Wright P, Phelan M, Stern J. *Core Psychiatry*. Philadelphia (PA): Harcourt Publishers Ltd, 2000.

AV. Bhugra D, Munro A, editors. *Troublesome Disguises: Underdiagnosed Psychiatric Syndromes*. Oxford: Blackwell Science, 1997.

AX. Rose NDB. *Essential Psychiatry*, 2nd edn. Oxford: Blackwell Science, 1996.

AY. Carlson NR, Buskist W, Martin NG. *Psychology: The Science of Behaviour*. European Adaptation. London: Allyn and Bacon, 1997

AZ. Appignanesi R, Zarate O. *Introducing Freud*. New York: Icon Books, 1998.

BA. Beck JS. *Cognitive Therapy: Basics and Beyond*. New York: The Guilford Press, 1995.

BC. Green B, editor. *The MRCPsych Study Manual*. Lancaster: Kluwer Academic Publishers, 1993.

BD. Walsh K. *Neuropsychology: a Clinical Approach*. 3rd edn. Edinburgh: Churchill Livingstone, 1994.

BE. Sackett DL, Straus SE Richardson SW, Rosenberg W, Brian Hynes R. *Evidence Based Medicine: How to Practice and Teach EBM*. 2nd edn. London: Churchill Livingstone, 2000.

BF. Emery AEH, Mueller RF. *Elements of Medical Genetics*. 8th edition. London: Churchill Livingstone, 1992.

BG. Bouras N, editor. *Psychiatric and Behavioural Disorders in Developmental Disabilities and Mental Retardation*. Cambridge: Cambridge University Press, 1999.

BH. Kelly C. *Alzheimer's Disease Handbook*. Basingstoke: Merit Publishing International, 2000.

BI. The Bethlem & Maudsley NHS Trust Prescribing Guidelines. 5th edn. London: Martin Dunitz, 1999.

BJ. Khoury MJ, Beaty TH, Cohen BH. *Fundamentals of Genetic Epidemiology*. Oxford: Oxford University Press, 1993.

BK. Jacob LS. *Pharmacology*. 3rd edn. Baltimore: Williams & Wilkins,

1992.

BL. Montgomery S, Rouillon F, editors. *Perspectives in Psychiatry*, Vol. 3: *Long-term treatment of Depression*. Chichester: John Wiley & Sons Ltd, 1992.

BM. Colbert D. *Fundamentals of Clinical Psychiatry*. London: Prentice Hall, 1993.

BN. Green JH. *An Introduction to Human Physiology*. 4th edn. Oxford: Oxford Medical Publications, 1991.

BO. Stevens A, Lowe J. *Human Histology*. 2nd edn. St. Louis (MO): Mosby Publications, 1994.

BP. Moore KL. *Clinically Oriented Anatomy*. 3rd edn. Baltimore: Williams & Wilkins, 1992.

BQ. Fitzgerald MJT. *Neuroanatomy: Basic and Clinical*. 2nd edn. London: Bailliere Tindall, 1992.

BR. Talley N, O'Connor S. *Clinical Examination*. 2nd edn. Oxford: Blackwell Science, 1995.

BS. Gillingham G. *Autism – Handle with Care*. 2nd edn. Arlington (TX): Future Horizons, 1997.

BT. Woods SK, Ploof WH. *Understanding ADHD: Attention Deficit Hyperactivity Disorder and the Feeling Brain*. London: Sage Publications, 1997.

BU. Murray RK. *Harper's Biochemistry*. 23rd edn. London: Prentice Hall, 1993.

BV. Briley M, Montgomery S, editors. *Antidepressant Therapy at the Dawn of the Third Millennium*. London: Martin Dunitz, 1998.

BW. Cahill DR. *Lachman's Case Studies in Anatomy*. 4th edn. Oxford: Oxford University Press, 1997.

BX. Dworetzky JP. *Psychology*. 4th edn. New York: West Publishing Company, 1991.

BY. Macionis JJ, Plummer K. *Sociology: A Global Introduction*. New Jersey: Prentice Hall, 1998.

BZ. Attwood T. *Asperger's Syndrome*. London: Jessica Kingsley Publishing, 1981.

CA. Ganong WF. *Review of Medical Physiology*. 16th International edn. New York: Appleton & Lange, 1993.

CB. Rabin BS. *Stress, Immune Function and Health: The Connection*. New York: John Wiley & Sons Inc, 1999.

CD. Batshaw M, editor. *Children with Disabilities*, 4th edn. Baltimore (MD): Brookes Publishing Co., 1997.

CE. Bouras N, editor. *Mental Health in Mental Retardation.* Cambridge: Cambridge University Press, 1994.

CF. Murray R, Hill P, McGuffin P, Birley JTL, editors. *The Essentials of Postgraduate Psychiatry.* 3rd edn. Cambridge: Cambridge University Press, 1997.

CG. Rutter M, Taylor E, Hersov L. *Child and Adolescent Psychiatry.* 3rd edn. Oxford: Blackwell Science, 1995.

CH. Graham P, Verhulst F, Turk F. *Child Psychiatry: A Developmental Approach.* 3rd edn. Oxford: Oxford University Press, 1999.

CI. Rycroft C. *A Critical Dictionary of Psychoanalysis.* 2nd edn. London: Penguin Books, 1995.

CJ. Bloch S. *An Introduction to the Psychotherapies* 3rd edn. Oxford: Oxford University Press, 1996.

CK. Hawton K, Heeringen K, editors. *The International Handbook of Suicide And Attempted Suicide.* Brisbane: John Wiley & Sons Ltd., 2000.

CL. Lee A, editor. *Recent Topics from Advances in Psychiatric Treatment: Volume 2.* London: Gaskell, 1999.

CM. Lawrie SM, McIntosh AM, Rao S. *Critical Appraisal for Psychiatry,* London: Churchill Livingstone, 2000.

CN. Jacobson JL, Jacobson AM. *Psychiatric Secrets.* Pennsylvania: Hanley and Belfus Inc, 1996.

CO. Faragher B, Marguerie C. *Essential Statistics for Medical Examinations.* Knutsford: Pastest, 1998.

CP. Coser LA, Nock SL, Steffan PA, Rhea B. *Introduction to Sociology.* 2nd edn. San Diego (CA): Harcourt Brace Jovanovich, 1987.

CQ. Thornicroft G, Szmukler G, editors. *Textbook of Community Psychiatry.* Oxford: Oxford University Press, 2001.

CR. Atkinson R, Atkinson R, Smith E, Bem D, Nolen-Hoeksema S. *Hilgards Introduction to Psychology,* 13th edn. London: Thomson Learning, 1999.

CS. Barker R, Barasi S, Neal MJ. *Neuroscience at a Glance.* Oxford: Blackwell Scientific, 1999.

CT. Westen D. *Psychology: Mind, Brain & Culture.* New York: John Wiley & Sons, 1996.

CU. Lawlor BA, editor. *Revision Psychiatry.* Dublin: MedMedia Ltd., 2001.

CV. Wallace H, Shovan SD. *Adults with Poorly Controlled Epilepsy: Clinical Guidelines for Treatment.* London: the Royal College of Physicians, 1997.

Stilnoct 5mg and 10mg tablets Prescribing Information - UK and Ireland Presentation: Stilnoct 10mg tablets contain 10mg zolpidem hemitartrate and Stilnoct 5mg tablets contain 5mg zolpidem hemitartrate. **Indication:** Short-term treatment of insomnia. A course of treatment should not exceed 4 weeks. **Dosage:** Tablets should be taken immediately before retiring, or in bed. Adults: one 10mg tablet. Elderly or debilitated patients: one 5mg tablet. Stilnoct should not be prescribed for children. **Contraindications:** Hypersensitivity to Stilnoct, obstructive sleep apnoea, myasthenia gravis, severe hepatic insufficiency, acute pulmonary insufficiency, respiratory depression or in psychotic illness. Stilnoct should not be prescribed for children. **Precautions and Warnings:** There is little evidence for the development of significant withdrawal-like symptoms, tolerance, rebound insomnia or abuse during the recommended treatment period, however, until further experience of use is gained, the prescribing physician should consider the possibility of their occurrence. No increases in dose were necessary during clinical trials to maintain clinical response, but the possibility of their occurrence should be considered. In studies, simulated vehicle driving is unaffected during the day following medication with Stilnoct, but there may be a possible risk of drowsiness the morning after therapy. Stilnoct should be administered with caution to patients with depression or a history of drug or alcohol abuse (although Stilnoct has not been shown to cause dependence). The effect of Stilnoct may be enhanced by other agents with central depressive activity e.g. alcohol, antihistamines, antidepressants. **Side Effects:** With doses up to 10mg, side effects included drowsiness, dizziness, diarrhoea, headache, nausea and vertigo. **Basic NHS Cost:** Stilnoct 10mg blister packs of 28 tablets £6.72. Stilnoct 5mg blister packs of 28 tablets £3.36. **Basic Cost in Ireland** Stilnoct 10mg blister packs of 28 tablets £6.70. Stilnoct 5mg blister packs of 28 tablets £3.35. **Legal Category:** POM. **Product Licence Numbers:** Stilnoct 10mg: PL4969/0027, Stilnoct 5mg: PL4969/0017. **Product Authorisation Numbers:** Stilnoct 5mg: PA 362/4/2, Stilnoct 10mg: PA 362/4/1. **Distributed in the Republic of Ireland by:** Allphar Services Ltd, Dublin. Tel: (01) 295 2226. **Product Licence Holder:** Lorex Synthélabo Ltd, Lunar House, Globe Park, Marlow, Bucks, SL7 1LW.

Lorex Synthélabo

Further information is available on request from:
Lorex Synthélabo Ltd, Lunar House,
Globe Park, Marlow,
Buckinghamshire, SL7 1LW

Lorex Synthélabo and Stilnoct are trade marks

STIL.142/February 1997

MCQs
in *Psychiatry*
for the
MRCPsych

MCQs
in *Psychiatry* for the
MRCPsych

by

Dr. Michael I. Levi MB BS MRCPsych
Consultant Psychiatrist
Lomond Healthcare NHS Trust
Vale of Leven District General Hospital
Alexandria, Dunbartonshire, Scotland, UK

 **PETROC PRESS**

Petroc Press, an imprint of LibraPharm Limited

Distributors

Plymbridge Distributors Limited, Plymbridge House, Estover Road, Plymouth PL6 7PZ, UK

Published in the United Kingdom by LibraPharm Limited, *Gemini House*, 162 Craven Road, Newbury, Berkshire RG14 5NR, UK

A catalogue record for this book is available from the British Library

ISBN 1 900603 85 3

Typeset by
Richard Powell Editorial and Production Services, Basingstoke, Hants
Printed and bound in the United Kingdom by
Hartnolls Limited, Bodmin, Cornwall

Contents

Foreword

Within psychiatry, the body of knowledge required to inform our management of patients is huge. Much can be learned through clinical practice in training and discussion with informed colleagues, but there is some knowledge which is established and about which discussion, as a way of testing a trainee's knowledge, is inappropriate.

The multiple-choice format is our college's way of examining knowledge of this kind over the whole range of psychiatry in a relatively economical way, and Dr Michael Levi is to be congratulated for continuing over the last ten years to provide the sample MCQs that psychiatric trainees need to prepare for their membership. He has gone to considerable trouble to offer teaching points in the answers sections.

It can be educational and entertaining to senior psychiatrists to dip into a book such as this in the knowledge that their trainees are very likely to ask their opinions!

David F. Gaskell BSc MB ChB MPhil MRCGP MRCPsych
Consultant Psychiatrist
Argyll and Bute Hospital
Lochgilphead
Argyll
Scotland
UK

January, 1997

Introduction

This book of multiple-choice questions in psychiatry consists of four papers, each containing fifty questions. The focus of the questions is on descriptive psychopathology as well as clinical topics in psychiatry. Extended answers to the questions follow each paper.

Each question consists of a main stem followed by five responses. The candidate must answer 'True' (T) or 'False' (F) to each response. The following marking scheme is in operation:

- A correctly answered response scores +1
- An incorrectly answered response scores −1
- An unanswered response scores 0

A score of 55% is regarded as satisfactory. The time allowed for each paper is ninety minutes.

The book will be useful to doctors preparing for either part of the MRCPsych, general practitioners and medical students. However, psychiatric nurses, psychiatric social workers, psychiatric occupational therapists and clinical psychologists will also find the book an asset.

9

Paper 1:   Questions

Q1. Autochthonous delusions are

A. synonymous with primary delusions
B. rarely preceded by a delusional atmosphere
C. a source of secondary delusions
D. pathognomonic of schizophrenia
E. 'brain waves'

Q2. Normal experiences include

A. jamais vu
B. delusional perception
C. derealisation
D. visual hallucinations
E. déjà vécu

Q3. Concrete thinking

A. is diagnostic of schizophrenia
B. is diagnostic of organic brain disease
C. may occur in manic-depressive psychosis
D. is a defect in conceptual abstract thought
E. is tested by interpretation of proverbs

Q4. Formication

A. is the medical term for fornication
B. may be seen in delirium
C. is a passivity phenomenon
D. is a tactile hallucination
E. may be called the 'cocaine bug'

Q5. Pseudohallucinations occur in

A. borderline syndrome
B. hypnagogic states
C. hypnopompic states
D. bereavement
E. fatigue

Q6.   Normal experiences include

A. hypnagogic hallucinations
B. hypnopompic hallucinations
C. depersonalisation
D. flight of ideas
E. over-inclusive thinking

Q7.   Jaspers described the following disorders of emotion

A. apathy
B. 'free-floating' emotions
C. loss of feeling
D. changes in bodily feelings
E. changes in feelings of competence

Q8.   Delusional perception

A. has two stages
B. is an autochthonous delusion
C. is often preceded by 'delusional mood'
D. occurs secondary to an hallucination
E. is a secondary delusion

Q9.   Pseudohallucinations

A. are subject to conscious manipulation
B. are dependent on environmental stimuli
C. may occur in the real world
D. may possess the vivid quality of normal perceptions
E. arise in inner space

Q10. Echolalia occurs in

A. catatonic schizophrenia
B. obsessional neurosis
C. mental handicap
D. manic-depressive psychosis
E. senile dementia

Q11. Formication

A. refers to actual insects crawling on the skin
B. occurs in 'delusions of infestation'
C. is seen when cocaine is withdrawn only
D. is a second-rank symptom of schizophrenia
E. is a disorder of thought content

Q12. Pathological excitement occurs in

A. retarded depression
B. manic-depressive psychosis
C. catatonic schizophrenia
D. delirium
E. normal subjects

Q13. The experience of depersonalisation is

A. usually pleasant
B. delusional
C. recognised as 'odd'
D. treatable with phenobarbitone
E. recognised as 'false'

Q14. The following statements are true

A. autoscopy is synonymous with phantom mirror-image
B. reflex hallucinations occur outside sensory field limits
C. functional hallucinations are experienced with their stimulus
D. in extra-campine hallucinations, a stimulus in one sensory field produces an hallucination in another
E. functional hallucinations are rare in chronic schizophrenia

Q15. Delusions

A. are held with a certainty that may be shakeable
B. are reality for the patient
C. are frequently held by other people
D. are rarely of personal significance
E. are usually of a bizarre nature

Q16. The following statements are true

A. mannerisms are non-goal-directed repetitive movements
B. stereotypes are goal-directed repetitive movements
C. opposition is an extreme form of negativism
D. athetosis consists of random, jerky movements
E. chorea consists of slow writhing movements

Q17. Sensory distortions include

A. macropsia
B. illusions
C. xanthopsia
D. pseudohallucinations
E. micropsia

Q18. Eidetic images

A. have been described by Taylor
B. are visual hallucinations
C. have never been perceived in relation to a real object
D. may be thought of as 'photographic memory'
E. are a form of exterocepted visual pseudohallucination

Q19. Pseudohallucinations occur in

A. dreams during sleep
B. lone prisoners
C. dreams whilst awake
D. long-distance lorry drivers
E. sensory deprivation

Q20. Verbigeration occurs in

A. extreme anxiety
B. the Ganser syndrome
C. senile dementia
D. malingering
E. catatonic schizophrenia

Q21. The following statements are true

A. delusions are ego-involved
B. redundancy refers to the predictability of a word appearing
C. delusions are idiosyncratic
D. schizophrenic thought has a high level of redundancy
E. paranoia is another term for paraphrenia

Q22. Neologisms occur in

A. manic-depressive psychosis
B. obsessive-compulsive disorder
C. organic brain disease
D. Gilles de la Tourette syndrome
E. schizophrenia

Q23. Verbigeration

A. may occur spontaneously
B. may be precipitated by comments of the questioner
C. is no different from echolalia
D. may be regarded as perseveration
E. is most common in schizophrenia

Q24. Negativism occurs in

A. senile dementia
B. simple schizophrenia
C. catatonic schizophrenia
D. severe mental handicap
E. 'active' and 'passive' forms

Q25. Circumstantiality occurs in

A. schizophrenia
B. epileptic personality changes
C. anxiety states
D. dullards
E. obsessional personalities

Q26. The following are true of Kurt and Carl Schneider

A. Kurt described fusion
B. Carl described thought broadcasting
C. they both described derailment
D. Kurt was Carl's step-sister
E. Carl described concrete thinking

Q27. Catalepsy is usually associated with

A. gegenhalten
B. echopraxia
C. flexibilitas cerea
D. cataplexy
E. waxy rigidity

Q28. Grandiose delusions occur in

A. mania
B. simple schizophrenia
C. Cotard's syndrome
D. Ekbom's syndrome
E. general paralysis of the insane

Q29. Euphoria occurs in

A. Cushing's syndrome
B. hebephrenic schizophrenia
C. disseminated sclerosis
D. thiamine deficiency
E. Pick's disease

Q30. Temporal disorientation occurs in

A. Wernicke's encephalopathy
B. hypomania
C. delirium
D. acute schizophrenia
E. dementia

Q31. Bleuler described the following

A. paraphrenia
B. paranoid schizophrenia
C. simple schizophrenia
D. schizoaffective disorders
E. paranoia

Q32. Types of receptive aphasias include

A. agnosic alexia
B. visual asymbolia
C. nominal aphasia
D. central aphasia
E. syntactical aphasia

Q33. Disorders of body schema include

A. autotopagnosia
B. gegenhalten
C. spasmodic torticollis
D. torpor
E. anosognosia

Q34. Disorders of adaptive movements include

A. automatic obedience
B. obstruction
C. mannerisms
D. stereotypes
E. tics

Q35. Sensory distortions include

A. dysmegalopsia
B. pareidolia
C. hypoacusis
D. hyperaesthesia
E. hallucinations

Q36. Abnormal expressions of emotion include

A. perplexity
B. apathy
C. emotional incontinence
D. emotional indifference
E. ecstasy

Q37. Echolalia and echopraxia occur in

A. catatonia
B. myriachit
C. cataplexy
D. latah
E. Gilles de la Tourette syndrome

Q38. Disorders of memory recognition include

A. primary delusional memories
B. Capgras syndrome
C. retrospective delusions
D. déjà vu
E. jamais vu

Q39. The borderline syndrome is characterised by

A. splitting
B. good impulse control
C. euphoric affect
D. primitive idealisation
E. feelings of emptiness

Q40. Recognised features of borderline personality disorder include

A. systematised delusions
B. projection
C. brief psychotic episodes
D. sublimation
E. ambivalent interpersonal relations

Q41. Somatic symptoms of severe anxiety include

A. impotence
B. diarrhoea
C. constipation
D. hypoventilation
E. sighing

Q42. Symptoms of anxiety include

A. smothering sensations
B. bradycardia
C. choking sensation
D. absence of sweating
E. dry mouth

Q43. Recognised features of the hyperventilation syndrome include

A. metabolic alkalosis
B. numbness of fingertips
C. respiratory acidosis
D. tingling of lips
E. increase in free ionised calcium

Q44. Recognised features of anxiety include

A. generalised autonomic arousal
B. little genetic predisposition
C. increased basal skin conductance
D. decreased plasma free fatty acids
E. hypotension and reflex tachycardia

Q45. Recognised features of anxiety neurosis include

A. burning on micturition
B. terminal insomnia
C. chest pain on exertion
D. extrasystoles
E. heartburn

Q46. Phobias have the following features

A. viewed as negative compulsions
B. can be reasoned away
C. fear proportional to the threat
D. described by Marks in 1929
E. involuntary

Q47. Agoraphobia is

A. better treated by flooding than systematic sensitisation
B. mainly seen in middle age
C. a fear specific to open spaces
D. more common in women
E. commonly associated with depersonalisation

Q48. Animal phobias are

A. more common in men
B. usually occur in middle age
C. generally non-specific
D. treatable with behaviour therapy
E. a poor diagnostic group

Q49. Social phobia

A. is usually specific to a few individuals
B. has an equal sex distribution
C. is as common as agoraphobia
D. usually develops before puberty
E. responds poorly to behavioural therapy

Q50. Folie du doute is characterised by

A. vacillation
B. delusions
C. indecisiveness
D. hallucinations
E. persistent doubting

Paper 1: Answers

A1.

A. T

B. F autochthonous or primary delusions are frequently preceded by a 'delusional mood', in which the patient feels something strange and threatening is happening, but is not sure exactly what

C. T

D. F autochthonous delusions are a Schneiderian first-rank symptom; definite evidence of first-rank symptoms indicates a diagnosis of schizophrenia, provided that there is no evidence of organic disorder or mania (first-rank symptoms occur in 10–20% of manic patients)

E. T

A2.

A. T

B. F delusional perception is one of Schneider's first-rank symptoms of schizophrenia

C. T

D. F visual hallucinations are associated particularly with organic mental disorders, but also occur in affective disorders and schizophrenia

E. T

A3.

A. F concrete thinking, that is difficulty in dealing with abstract ideas, is a clinical feature of schizophrenia but not diagnostic of it

B. F

C. T

D. T

E. T

A4.

A. F
B. T
C. F formication ('cocaine bugs') is characteristic of cocaine depend-
      ence. It is a bizarre tactile hallucination in which there is a
      feeling as though insects are crawling under the skin
D. T
E. T

A5.

A. F patients with the borderline syndrome may have brief psychotic
      episodes involving hallucinations
B. T
C. T
D. T
E. T

A6.

A. T
B. T
C. T
D. F flight of ideas are most characteristically seen in hypomania
E. F over-inclusive thinking is most characteristically seen in schizo-
      phrenia

A7.

A. T
B. T
C. T
D. T
E. T

A8.

A. T
B. T
C. T
D. F delusional perception is a false belief which arises fully formed
      as a sudden intuition, having no discernible connection with any
      previous interactions or experiences
E. F delusional perception is a primary delusion

A9.

A. F
B. F
C. F
D. F
E. T pseudohallucinations are perceived as being located in subjective space, i.e. within the mind

A10.

A. T echolalia is the repetition by the patient of the interviewer's words or phrases. It is a motor disorder of general behaviour
B. F
C. T
D. F
E. T

A11.

A. F
B. F
C. F
D. F
E. F

A12.

A. F pathological depression occurs
B. T
C. T
D. T
E. F normal excitement occurs

A13.

A. F
B. F
C. T depersonalisation is a change in self-awareness such that the person feels unreal
D. F
E. T

A14.

A. T
B. F in reflex hallucinations, a stimulus in one sensory field produces an hallucination in another

C. T
D. F extra-campine hallucinations occur outside sensory field limits
E. F

A15.

A. F
B. T delusions are false beliefs with the following characteristics: firmly held despite evidence to the contrary; out of keeping with the person's educational and cultural background; content often bizarre; often infused with a sense of great personal meaning
C. F
D. F
E. T

A16.

A. F
B. F
C. F
D. F
E. F

A17.

A. T
B. F illusions are sensory deceptions
C. T
D. F pseudohallucinations are sensory deceptions
E. T

A18.

A. T
B. F
C. F
D. T eidetic images are a form of pseudohallucination. Previous perceptions are reproduced as mental images of uncanny detail and vivid intensity
E. T

A19.

A. F pseudohallucinations occur when falling asleep (hypnagogic hallucinations) or when waking up (hypnopompic hallucinations)
B. T
C. T
D. T
E. T

A20.

A. T verbigeration is the disruption of both the connection between topics and the finer grammatical structure of speech

B. F

C. T

D. F

E. T

A21.

A. T

B. T

C. T

D. F schizophrenic thought has a low level of redundancy

E. F in paranoia delusions are present, hallucinations are absent and personality is intact; in paraphrenia delusions are present, hallucinations are present and personality is intact

A22.

A. T

B. F neologisms are words or phrases used by the patient which are invented by himself; they do not occur in obsessive-compulsive disorder

C. T

D. T

E. T

A23.

A. T

B. T

C. F

D. F perseveration is the persistent and inappropriate repetition of the same thoughts

E. T

A24.

A. T negativism is a motor disorder of general behaviour in which there is an apparently motiveless resistance to suggestion or attempts at movement

B. F

C. T

D. T

E. T

A25.

A. F
B. T circumstantiality is the incorporation of trivial detail such that the individual is slow to get to the point
C. F
D. T
E. T

A26.

A. F
B. F
C. F
D. F
E. F

A27.

A. F
B. F
C. T catalepsy (also called waxy flexibility) is a motor disorder of general behaviour in which the patient's limbs can be placed in an awkward posture and remain fixed in position over a long period, despite asking the patient to relax
D. F
E. T

A28.

A. T
B. F delusions do not occur
C. F nihilistic delusions occur
D. F hypochondriacal delusions occur
E. T

A29.

A. T
B. T
C. T
D. T
E. T

A30.

A. T
B. F cognitive function including orientation is intact in functional psychiatric disorders

C. T
D. F
E. T

A31.

A. F
B. T
C. T
D. F   described by Kasanin
E. F

A32.

A. T
B. T
C. F   an intermediate aphasia associated with the inability to name objects, in spite of the individual having a large vocabulary at his disposal
D. F   an intermediate aphasia associated with difficulty with both the receptive and expressive aspects of speech. Synonymous with syntactical aphasia
E. F

A33.

A. T
B. F   a motor disorder of general behaviour
C. F   an acute dystonic reaction
D. F
E. T

A34.

A. F   a disorder of induced non-adaptive movements
B. T
C. T
D. F   a disorder of spontaneous non-adaptive movements
E. F   a disorder of spontaneous non-adaptive movements

A35.

A. T
B. F   a special type of illusion, vivid mental images occurring without conscious effort when perceiving an ill-defined stimulus, e.g. the subject sees pictures in a glowing fire. It is therefore a sensory deception
C. T

D. T
E. F a sensory deception

A36.

A. T
B. F an abnormal emotional reaction
C. T
D. T
E. F an abnormal emotional reaction

A37.

A. T
B. T
C. F cataplexy is a clinical feature of narcolepsy and it involves a sudden reduction in muscle tone; the patient may fall to the ground
D. T
E. T

A38.

A. F a disorder of memory recall
B. T
C. F a disorder of memory recall
D. T
E. T

A39.

A. T
B. F poor impulse control
C. F variable moods
D. T
E. T

A40.

A. F
B. T
C. T
D. F the ego-defence mechanisms associated with borderline personality disorder are splitting and projective identification
E. T

A41.

A. T
B. T
C. T
D. F   hyperventilation
E. T

A42.

A. T
B. F   tachycardia
C. T
D. F   sweating present
E. T

A43.

A. F   metabolic acidosis
B. T
C. F   respiratory alkalosis
D. T
E. F   decrease in free ionised calcium

A44.

A. F
B. F   evidence for a genetic aetiology is provided by both family
studies and twin studies
C. T
D. F   increased plasma free fatty acids
E. F

A45.

A. F   increased frequency and urgency of micturition
B. F   initial insomnia
C. F   feeling of discomfort or pain over the heart at rest
D. T
E. T

A46.

A. T
B. F   cannot be reasoned away
C. F   fear out of proportion to the threat
D. F   described by Marks in 1969
E. T

A47.

A. T
B. T
C. F often used for a fear of shops, supermarkets, buses, trains, crowds and any place that cannot be left suddenly without attracting attention, e.g. a seat in the middle of a row in the theatre
D. T
E. T

A48.

A. F more common in women
B. F onset in childhood
C. F usually specific phobias
D. T
E. F

A49.

A. F
B. F T (M) = (F)
C. F
D. F
E. F

A50.

A. T
B. F psychotic symptoms do not occur
C. T
D. F
E. T

Paper 2: Questions

Q1. Obsessional thoughts

A. always give rise to compulsions
B. are ego-alien
C. are rarely of a sexual nature
D. are best treated by thought stopping
E. usually respond to imipramine

Q2. Obsessive rituals

A. respond well to behaviour therapy
B. are usually anti-social
C. are not resisted
D. are sensibly regarded
E. reduce anxiety

Q3. Recognised features of obsessional thoughts include

A. a subjective sense of compulsion
B. blasphemy as a common theme
C. an aggressive theme frequently translated into violence
D. the intrusion of foreign thoughts into the mind
E. resistance associated with reduced anxiety

Q4. Recognised features of obsessional thoughts include

A. ego-dystonic
B. ego-alien
C. may be enjoyable to patient
D. usually in a foreign language
E. respond well to neuroleptics

Q5. Obsessional symptoms occur in

A. early dementia
B. encephalitis lethargica
C. anorexia nervosa
D. post-encephalitic parkinsonism
E. head injury

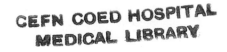

Q6. In Briquet's syndrome

A. there is usually an organic basis
B. recurrence is unusual
C. somatic complaints are usually multiple
D. the prognosis is excellent
E. surgery is the treatment of choice

Q7. Dissociative states

A. occur in hysteria
B. may be seen under hypnosis
C. include fugue states
D. exclude multiple personalities
E. are seen in petit-mal seizures

Q8. Briquet's syndrome

A. is allied to hysteria
B. occurs in men
C. is synonymous with somatisation disorder
D. has a prevalence of 1–2% in women
E. has sexual symptoms infrequently

Q9. Recognised features of the Ganser syndrome include

A. verbigeration
B. pseudohallucinations
C. ataxia
D. dissociative amnesia
E. vorbeireden

Q10. Recognised features of the Munchausen syndrome include

A. named by Professor Munchausen in the 18th century
B. never presents with psychiatric symptoms
C. may present with false bereavements
D. rarely accompanied by alcohol dependence
E. easy to treat

Q11. Recognised features of the Ganser syndrome include

A. described by Ganser in 1890
B. also known as 'the buffoonery syndrome'
C. also known as 'prison psychosis'
D. no specific therapy
E. pseudohallucinations commonly

Q12. Recognised features of the couvade syndrome include

A. a pregnant husband
B. ambivalence
C. very rare
D. identification
E. defined by Trethowan in 1955

Q13. Hysterical conversion symptoms include

A. convulsions
B. specific EEG changes
C. aphonia
D. akathisia
E. pupillary dilatation

Q14. Risk groups for hypochondriasis include

A. females
B. Jewish people
C. higher social classes
D. the elderly
E. medical students

Q15. The Capgras syndrome

A. is allied to hysteria
B. usually is associated with organic brain disease
C. is also called 'pure erotomania'
D. is characterised by a pregnant husband
E. is also called 'delusion of doubles'

Q16. In folie à deux

A. most patients are not blood relatives
B. 50% of patients recover on mere separation
C. brothers are most commonly affected
D. the psychopathology is different from folie à plusiers
E. the delusions are usually persecutory

Q17. Recognised features of de Clérambault's syndrome include

A. equal sex incidence
B. a 'pure' form of the syndrome
C. most commonly seen in hebephrenia
D. a belief typically founded on platonic love
E. the patient rarely desires a sexual relationship

Q18. Associations of morbid jealousy include

A. paranoia
B. overt homosexuality
C. organic psychosis
D. obsessional personality
E. feelings of inadequacy

Q19. Recognised features of the Capgras syndrome include

A. usually is associated with schizophrenia
B. occurs frequently
C. rarely accompanies a paranoid psychosis
D. the spouse is often implicated
E. may be based on a real imposter

Q20. Recognised features of the Capgras syndrome include

A. splitting
B. usually associated with affective disorders
C. projection
D. usually associated with non-relatives
E. also called l'illusion des sosies

Q21. Associations of morbid jealousy include

A. personality disorders
B. schizophrenia
C. manic-depressive psychosis
D. obsessional neurosis
E. hysteria

Q22. Associations of morbid jealousy include

A. Parkinson's disease
B. cocainism
C. dementia
D. general paralysis of the insane
E. cerebral tumour

Q23. Recognised features of de Clérambault's syndrome include

A. originally described in a pure form
B. a paranoid state
C. a manic state
D. similar to Ekbom's syndrome
E. similar to Othello syndrome

Q24. Psychotic depression is characterised by

A. delusions of illness
B. jamais vu
C. visual hallucinations
D. nihilistic delusions
E. circumstantiality

Q25. Depressive psychosis is characterised by

A. delusions of filth
B. delusions of poverty
C. delusions of guilt
D. primary delusions
E. auditory hallucinations

Q26. Pseudodementia is characterised by

A. onset with depressive features
B. abnormal EEG
C. presence of localising neurological signs
D. past or family history of manic-depressive psychosis
E. chronic course

Q27. Recognised features of hypomania include

A. hypersomnia
B. grandiose delusions
C. wise business investments
D. decreased libido
E. poverty of thought

Q28. Anaclitic depression is characterised by

A. infants deprived of mother in early life
B. initial vigorous protest
C. severe despair
D. a phase of detachment
E. a predisposition to manic-depressive psychosis

Q29. Recognised features of mania include

A. rhyming
B. transient depression
C. clang associations
D. passivity phenomena
E. punning

Q30. Recognised features of endogenous depression include

A. amenorrhoea
B. visual hallucinations
C. constipation
D. urinary incontinence
E. may be called psychotic depression

Q31. Associations of psychotic depressives with obsessions include

A. self-reproach
B. less prone to suicide
C. diurnal variation in mood
D. increased libido
E. depersonalisation

Q32. Depressive disorder may present as

A. hysterical conversion
B. schizophrenia
C. an anxiety state
D. shop-lifting
E. hypochondriasis

Q33. Recognised features of mania include

A. thought broadcasting
B. expansiveness
C. somatic passivity
D. physical underactivity
E. 'made' affect

Q34. Predictors of good response to amitriptyline include

A. lower socioeconomic class
B. middle insomnia
C. multiple prior episodes of depression
D. late insomnia
E. anorexia

Q35. Recognised features of mania include

A. infectious humour
B. real suicidal risk
C. anger
D. hallucinations
E. periods of depression

Q36. Recognised features of hypomania include

A. sustained cheerfulness
B. sadness
C. quick temper
D. sustained affability
E. insidious onset

Q37. Formal thought disorder includes

A. drivelling
B. condensation
C. flight of ideas
D. perseveration
E. transitory thinking

Q38. Recognised features of catatonic schizophrenia include

A. forced grasping
B. mitgehen
C. athetosis
D. palilalia
E. logoclonia

Q39. First-rank symptoms of schizophrenia

A. are always pathognomonic of schizophrenia
B. include 2nd and 3rd party hallucinations
C. incorporate all passivity phenomena
D. exclude formal thought disorder
E. include incongruity of affect

Q40. In the double-blind situation

A. two conflicting messages are given simultaneously
B. experimental evidence is provided for schizophrenia
C. a double-bind situation also occurs
D. comments on the situation itself are permitted
E. both messages are always verbal

Q41. Simple schizophrenia is characterised by

A. hallucinations
B. insidious onset
C. gradual deterioration
D. social isolation
E. delusions

Q42. Passivity experiences

A. include made actions
B. occur in manic-depressive psychosis
C. include echo de la pensée
D. are recognised in obsessional neurosis
E. exclude thought broadcasting

Q43. The following statements are true in schizophrenia

A. schism describes hostility between parents
B. skew describes a dominant mother and submissive father
C. invalidation describes denial of feelings of family members
D. praecox feeling refers to empathic rapport with the patient
E. pseudomutuality is a method by which a family system maintains
   equilibrium

Q44. Evidence for formal thought disorder includes

A. inflexibility of personal constructs
B. knight's move thinking
C. loosening of personal constructs
D. nominal aphasia
E. a normal repertory grid

Q45. Schizophrenic thought disorder includes

A. 'woolly' thinking
B. blurring of conceptual boundaries
C. paranoid delusions
D. omission
E. substitutions

Q46. The following associations are correct

A. Cameron and concrete thinking
B. Schneider and condensation
C. Bleuler and drivelling
D. Goldstein and over-inclusive thinking
E. Bleuler and loosening of associations

Q47. Passivity experiences include

A. thought block
B. echopraxia
C. 'made' volitions
D. obsessional rituals
E. voices commenting on the individual in the third person

Q48. Schneider's first-rank symptoms include

A. delusional mood
B. sudden delusional idea
C. delusional perception
D. flattened affect
E. thought block

Q49. Auditory hallucinations typical of schizophrenia include

A. gedankenlautwerden
B. schnauzkrampf
C. vorbeireden
D. echo de la pensée
E. mitgehen

Q50. Stupor occurs in

A. mania
B. depression
C. hysteria
D. petit-mal epilepsy
E. Gjessing's periodic catatonia

Paper 2: Answers

A1.

A. F compulsions do not always arise
B. T
C. F often are of a sexual, violent or blasphemous nature
D. F are best treated by exposure and response prevention when occurring with rituals. In the absence of rituals, obsessional thoughts are best treated by medication
E. F usually respond to selective serotonin reuptake inhibitors, e.g. fluoxetine

A2.

A. F
B. F
C. F are resisted
D. F are regarded as absurd
E. T

A3.

A. T
B. T
C. F
D. F the patient regards the thoughts as alien (ego-alien), while recognising them as the product of his own mind (ego-syntonic)
E. F

A4.

A. F ego-syntonic
B. T
C. T
D. F
E. F

A5.

A. T
B. T
C. T
D. T
E. T

A6.

A. F there is no organic basis
B. F
C. T
D. F the prognosis is poor
E. F

A7.

A. T
B. T
C. T
D. F include multiple personalities
E. F are not seen in petit-mal seizures

A8.

A. T
B. T
C. T
D. T
E. F has sexual symptoms frequently

A9.

A. F vorbeireden – the giving of approximate answers, i.e. answers to
       simple questions that are plainly wrong but strongly suggest that
       the correct answer is known
B. T
C. T
D. T
E. T

A10.

A. F the syndrome is not named after Professor Munchausen
B. F may present with psychiatric symptoms
C. T
D. F often accompanied by alcohol dependence
E. F difficult to treat

A11.

A. F described by Ganser in 1897
B. F may be similar to the 'buffoonery state' of acute or catatonic schizophrenia
C. T
D. T
E. F pseudohallucinations occasionally

A12.

A. F the husband of a pregnant woman experiences some of the symptoms of pregnancy
B. T
C. F rare
D. T
E. F

A13.

A. T
B. F there is no organic basis
C. T
D. F an extra-pyramidal side-effect of antipsychotic drugs
E. F blindness

A14.

A. F males
B. T
C. F lower social classes
D. T
E. T

A15.

A. F usually associated with affective disorders or schizophrenia
B. F rarely associated with organic disorders
C. F 'pure erotomania' is the 'pure' form of de Clérambault's syndrome
D. F
E. T

A16.

A. F most patients are blood relatives
B. F separation sometimes leads to the disappearance of the delusional state, improvement being more likely in the recipient than the inducer. If identifiable, the psychotic member needs

treatment with anti-psychotic medication
C. F
D. F they share the same psychopathology
E. T

A17.

A. F the subject is usually a single woman
B. T
C. F usually associated with paranoid schizophrenia
D. F a delusional belief that another person (the object), often of unattainably higher social status, loves the patient (the subject) intensely
E. F the subject believes that the object is unable to reveal his love to her. The subject may be importunate and disrupt the object's life

A18.

A. T
B. F may be projection of repressed homosexuality
C. T
D. T
E. T

A19.

A. T
B. F
C. F
D. T
E. F a delusion in which a patient sees a familiar person and believes him to have been replaced by an impostor, who is an exact double of the original person

A20.

A. T
B. T
C. T
D. F usually associated with close relatives, particularly the spouse
E. T

A21.

A. T
B. T
C. T
D. T
E. T

A22.

A. T
B. T
C. T
D. T
E. T

A23.

A. T
B. T
C. T
D. F in Ekbom's syndrome, the essential feature is a delusion in which a patient believes his skin is infected by insects
E. F in the Othello syndrome, the essential feature is a delusion in which a patient believes that the marital partner is being unfaithful

A24.

A. T
B. F may occur in neurological disorders
C. F associated particularly with organic mental disorders
D. T
E. F frequently seen in hypomania

A25.

A. T
B. T
C. T
D. F characteristic of schizophrenia
E. T

A26.

A. T
B. F normal EEG
C. F absence of focal signs
D. T
E. F relatively acute onset

A27.

A. F insomnia
B. T
C. F unwise business investments
D. F increased libido
E. F pressure of thought

A28.

A. T
B. T
C. T
D. T
E. F   there is no such predisposition

A29.

A. T
B. T
C. T
D. T
E. T

A30.

A. T
B. T
C. T
D. F   constipation is a recognised feature
E. T

A31.

A. T
B. T
C. T
D. F   decreased libido
E. T

A32.

A. T
B. F   in the diagnostic hierarchy, schizophrenia is a higher priority
        condition than depressive disorder, i.e. schizophrenia may
        present as a depressive disorder
C. T
D. T
E. T

A33.

A. T
B. T
C. T   schneiderian first-rank symptoms of schizophrenia occur in 10–
        20% of manic patients
D. F   physical overactivity
E. T

A34.

A. **F** does not predict response
B. **T**
C. **F**
D. **T**
E. **T**

A35.

A. **T**
B. **T**
C. **T**
D. **T**
E. **T**

A36.

A. **F** mood is one of euphoria with infectious gaiety, but may be interrupted by brief episodes of depression. Anger and irritability also occur
B. **T**
C. **T**
D. **F**
E. **F** acute onset

A37.

A. **T**
B. **T**
C. **T**
D. **T**
E. **T**

A38.

A. **F**
B. **T** an extreme form of mitmachen in which the patient will move in any direction with very slight pressure
C. **F** slow, writhing, semi-rotatory movements
D. **T**
E. **T**

A39.

A. **F** definite evidence indicates a diagnosis of schizophrenia, provided that there is no evidence of an organic disorder
B. **F** Second party hallucinations are second-rank symptoms of schizophrenia

C. T
D. T
E. F incongruity of affect is a second-rank symptom of schizophrenia

A40.

A. F
B. F
C. F
D. F
E. F

A41.

A. F hallucinations are absent
B. T
C. T
D. T
E. F delusions are absent

A42.

A. T
B. T
C. F in echo de la pensée, the patient experiences a voice repeating his own thoughts immediately after he has thought them
D. F
E. F include thought broadcasting

A43.

A. T
B. T
C. T
D. T
E. T

A44.

A. F
B. T
C. T
D. F
E. F evidence includes an abnormally loose personal construct system, which can be measured with the repertory grid

A45.

A. T
B. T
C. F disorder of thought content
D. T
E. T

A46.

A. F Cameron is associated with over-inclusive thinking
B. F Schneider is associated with drivelling
C. F Bleuler is associated with condensation
D. F Goldstein is associated with concrete thinking
E. T

A47.

A. F disorder of the stream of thought
B. F a motor disorder of general behaviour
C. T
D. F
E. F

A48.

A. F
B. F
C. T
D. F flattened or blunted affect is a Schneiderian second-rank system
E. F

A49.

A. T in gedankenlautwerden, the patient experiences a voice speaking
     his own thoughts as he thinks them
B. F
C. F
D. T
E. F

A50.

A. T
B. T
C. F
D. T
E. T

Paper 3: Questions

Q1. Predictors of good prognosis in schizophrenia include

A. lack of precipitating factors
B. insidious onset
C. presence of affective symptoms
D. good premorbid personality
E. negative family history of an affective illness

Q2. Recognised features of double-bind situations include

A. a setting of emotional arousal
B. two adults involved in communication
C. usually only one message
D. parents rarely involved in communication
E. a placebo

Q3. Recognised features of chronic schizophrenia include

A. formal thought disorder
B. delusional perception
C. behavioural slowing
D. incongruity of affect
E. cognitive slowing

Q4. Bleuler's secondary/accessory symptoms of schizophrenia include

A. delusions
B. ambivalence
C. hallucinations
D. emotional flattening
E. catatonic symptoms

Q5. High prevalence rates of schizophrenia occur in

A. southern Irish
B. north-west Croatians
C. Roman Catholic Canadians
D. northern Irish
E. Hutterites

Q6.   Positive symptoms of schizophrenia include

A. diminished volition
B. derailment
C. age disorientation
D. incongruity of affect
E. delusional perception

Q7.   Carl Schneider described the following

A. thought echo
B. 'made' experiences
C. thought broadcasting
D. 'second-rank' symptoms of schizophrenia
E. delusional perception

Q8.   Bleuler's 'four A´s' of schizophrenia include

A. autochthonous delusions
B. flattening of affect
C. loosening of association
D. third person auditory hallucinations
E. withdrawal (autism)

Q9.   Schizophrenic thought disorder includes

A. primary delusions
B. asyndesis
C. obsessional thoughts
D. metonymy
E. perseveration

Q10.   Schizophreniform psychosis occurs in

A. myxoedema
B. thiamine deficiency
C. Economo's encephalitis
D. phaeochromocytoma
E. Wilson's disease

Q11. In organic disturbance of mental state

A. verbal IQ falls off before performance
B. concrete thinking is unusual
C. derealisation occurs
D. there is altered level of consciousness
E. visual hallucinations occur

Q12. Delirium tremens is characterised by

A. clouding of consciousness
B. visual illusions
C. lilliputian hallucinations
D. olfactory illusions
E. auditory illusions

Q13. Bromism may present with

A. hypomania
B. auditory and visual hallucinations
C. delusions
D. depression
E. bad breath

Q14. The dysmnesic syndrome features

A. paranoid delusions
B. delusional perception
C. ataxia
D. peripheral neuropathy
E. long-term memory impairment

Q15. In Huntington's chorea

A. athetoid movements are usual presenting signs
B. gross personality change is very unusual
C. children have a less rapid deterioration
D. the onset of symptoms is usually in childhood
E. 75% of an affected person's children develop the disease

Q16. Recognised features of the Gilles de la Tourette syndrome include

A. echolalia
B. coprolalia
C. coprophagia
D. flatus
E. echopraxia

Q17. Recognised features of Pick's disease include

A. fatuous mood
B. apathy
C. general euphoria
D. a frequently abnormal EEG
E. preservation of intellect

Q18. Recognised features of Alzheimer's disease include

A. anxious mood
B. depression
C. specific abnormalities on EEG
D. a deficiency of GABA
E. a deficiency of serotonin

Q19. Complications of chronic alcoholism include

A. paraesthesia and pain in the extremities
B. an abnormal pyruvate tolerance test
C. weakness of the limbs
D. osteoporosis
E. a decrease in erythrocyte transketolase activity

Q20. Recognised features of the alcohol withdrawal state include

A. depression
B. nausea
C. choking feeling
D. fits
E. autonomic underactivity

Q21. Recognised features of the amotivational syndrome include

A. occurs in heavy cocaine users
B. self-neglect
C. good initiative
D. hallucinations
E. social deterioration

Q22. Possible risk groups for alcoholism include

A. Jewish people
B. Irish people
C. journalists
D. doctors
E. Catholic priests

Q23. Recognised features of alcoholic hallucinosis include

A. visual hallucinations
B. clear consciousness
C. Korsakoff's psychosis
D. cessation of drinking usually causes improvement
E. some patients turn out to be schizophrenic

Q24. Recognised features of normal pressure hydrocephalus include

A. lack of spontaneity
B. hypotonic limbs
C. psychomotor responses
D. Babinski's responses
E. urinary retention

Q25. Psychiatric sequelae of severe head injuries include

A. neurotic symptoms
B. psychoses
C. personality changes
D. apathy
E. emotional lability

Q26. Recognised features of multi-infarct dementia include

A. insidious onset
B. early deterioration of personality
C. depression
D. global deterioration of intellectual faculties
E. lability of mood

Q27. Recognised features of the frontal-lobe syndrome include

A. poverty of speech
B. receptive dysphasia
C. depression
D. tactful behaviour
E. epilepsy

Q28. Recognised features of hypothyroidism include

A. organic psychosis
B. delirium
C. depressive psychosis
D. dementia
E. schizophreniform psychosis

Q29. Recognised features of multiple sclerosis include

A. euphoria
B. dementia
C. cerebellar signs
D. depressive ideation
E. grandiose delusions

Q30. Associations of epilepsy include

A. hysteria
B. hypersexuality
C. depression
D. anxiety
E. personality disorders

Q31. Recognised features of Huntington's chorea include

A. choreiform movements always precede dementia
B. distractability only occasionally
C. epilepsy
D. depression
E. paranoid state

Q32. Recognised features of Cushing's syndrome include

A. euphoria
B. depression
C. anxiety
D. delusions
E. hallucinations

Q33. Organic sequelae of alcoholism include

A. increased incidence of myocardial infarction
B. pneumonia
C. folate deficiency
D. cardiomyopathy
E. oesophageal varices

Q34. Recognised features of vitamin B_{12} deficiency include

A. depression
B. mania
C. dementia
D. paranoid states
E. confusional episodes

Q35. Recognised features of Wernicke's encephalopathy include

A. confabulation
B. ataxia
C. Korsakoff's psychosis
D. peripheral neuropathy
E. staggering gait

Q36. Recognised features of Alzheimer's disease include

A. onset at age 60–70 years
B. amnesia is rarely the first symptom noted
C. EEG changes usually seen in late stages of illness
D. marked loss of verbal skills on WAIS
E. psychotic features

Q37. Recognised features of the punch-drunk syndrome include

A. pyramidal lesions
B. preservation of intellect
C. extrapyramidal lesions
D. decreased tolerance of alcohol
E. senile plaques

Q38. Recognised features of delirium include

A. illusions
B. nocturnal worsening
C. misidentifications
D. paranoid delusions
E. non-fluctuating course

Q39. Recognised features of Gerstmann's syndrome include

A. visual agnosia
B. dyspraxia
C. dysfunction of non-dominant parietal lobe
D. Ganser's syndrome
E. dyscalculia

Q40. Recognised features of non-dominant parietal-lobe dysfunction include

A. right-left disorientation
B. witzelsucht
C. sensory Jacksonian fits
D. astereognosis
E. anosognosia

Q41. Recognised features of Pick's disease include

A. 'frontal lobe' syndrome
B. the 'gramophone' symptom
C. memory deficits occurring early
D. personality deterioration occurring later
E. more common in men

Q42. Recognised features of head injury include

A. retrograde amnesia is a good prognostic indicator
B. personality change is the commonest psychiatric sequela
C. it may lead to normal pressure hydrocephalus
D. epilepsy occurs in 5% of open head injuries
E. cognitive impairment occurs in 30% of severe injuries

Q43. Recognised features of hypopituitarism include

A. coma
B. delirium
C. apathy
D. irritability
E. cognitive impairment

Q44. Recognised features of delirium tremens include

A. hypomagnesaemia
B. hypersomnia
C. autonomic underactivity
D. hyperkalaemia
E. hunger

Q45. Recognised features of Korsakoff's psychosis include

A. spatial disorientation
B. brisk reflexes
C. temporal disorientation
D. flattening of affect
E. anterograde amnesia

Q46. Recognised features of the temporal-lobe syndrome include

A. ideational apraxia
B. alexia
C. hemisomatognosia
D. aggressive behaviour
E. topographical agnosia

Q47. Recognised features of the Klüver–Bucy syndrome include

A. memory impairment
B. visual agnosis
C. hypo-orality
D. rage
E. hyposexuality

Q48. Recognised features of frontal-lobe syndrome include

A. lack of foresight
B. cortical sensory loss
C. finger agnosia
D. receptive dysphasia
E. memory loss

Q49. Associations of temporal-lobe epilepsy include

A. depersonalisation
B. cerebral tumour
C. gustatory hallucinations
D. lip smacking
E. derealisation

Q50. Mirror gazing occurs in

A. anorexia nervosa
B. manic-depressive psychosis
C. hebephrenia
D. obsessional neurosis
E. senile dementia

Paper 3: Answers

A1.

A. F   presence of a precipitating factor
B. F   acute onset
C. T
D. T
E. F   prominence of affective symptoms

A2.

A. T
B. F   a parent and their child involved in communication
C. F   two conflicting and incompatible messages
D. F
E. F   this features in double-blind placebo controlled clinical trials

A3.

A. T
B. F   acute schizophrenia
C. T
D. F   acute schizophrenia
E. T

A4.

A. T
B. F   Bleuler's primary/fundamental symptom of schizophrenia
C. T
D. F   Bleuler's primary/fundamental symptom of schizophrenia
E. T

A5.

A. T
B. T
C. T
D. F   high prevalence rate of schizophrenia in southern Irish
E. F   low prevalence rate of schizophrenia in Hutterites

A6.

A. F negative symptom of schizophrenia
B. F negative symptom of schizophrenia; derailment is one form of schizophrenic thought disorder
C. F negative symptom of schizophrenia; age disorientation is present if the patient can correctly give his date of birth and the current date, but gives a gross underestimate of his current age
D. T
E. T

A7.

A. F
B. F
C. F
D. F
E. F

A8.

A. F Bleuler's secondary/accessory symptom of schizophrenia
B. T
C. T
D. F Bleuler's secondary/accessory symptom of schizophrenia
E. T

A9.

A. F
B. T
C. F
D. T
E. F perseveration is a disorder of the form of thought occurring in acute and chronic organic disorders; it refers to the persistent and inappropriate repetition of the same thoughts

A10.

A. T
B. F Korsakoff's psychosis occurs in thiamine deficiency
C. T
D. F anxiety symptoms occur in phaeochromocytoma
E. T

A11.

A. F performance IQ falls off before verbal
B. F concrete thinking is not unusual

C. T
D. T
E. T

A12.

A. T
B. T
C. T in delirium tremens, illusions may progress to frightening hallu-
cinations, which are most commonly visual hallucinations, but
may also be auditory or tactile hallucinations
D. F
E. T

A13.

A. T
B. T
C. T
D. T
E. T

A14.

A. F a feature of delirium tremens
B. F a Schneiderian first-rank symptom of schizophrenia
C. T
D. T
E. F impairment of recent memory

A15.

A. F
B. F
C. F
D. F
E. F

A16.

A. T echolalia is the repetition by the patient of the interviewer's
words or phrases
B. T coprolalia refers to explosive obscene utterances by the patient
C. F coprophagia is the oral ingestion of faeces by the patient
D. F
E. T echopraxia is the imitation by the patient of the interviewer's
movements

A17.

A. T
B. T
C. T
D. F
E. F   decreased intellectual drive

A18.

A. T
B. T
C. F
D. T
E. F   dopamine-β-hydroxylase reduced in early onset cases; degeneration of acetylcholine neurones with a selective reduction in choline acetyltransferase and acetylcholinesterase enzymic activity

A19.

A. T
B. T
C. T
D. T
E. T

A20.

A. T
B. T
C. T
D. T
E. F   autonomic overactivity

A21.

A. F   heavy cannabis users
B. T
C. F   blunted motivation, i.e. apathy, decreased drive, lack of ambition
D. F   psychotic reactions are an adverse effect of cannabis in patients with a pre-existing psychosis or a vulnerability to psychosis; they are not part of the amotivational syndrome
E. T

A22.

A. F   less common in Jewish people
B. T

C. T
D. T
E. F

A23.

A. F auditory hallucinations
B. T
C. F a nutritional alcohol-related psychiatric disorder due to a sustained
      lack of thiamine; this is unrelated to alcoholic hallucinosis
D. T
E. T

A24.

A. T
B. F
C. T
D. F
E. F urinary incontinence

A25.

A. T
B. T
C. T
D. T
E. T

A26.

A. F acute onset with stepwise deterioration in memory
B. F personality preservation until late
C. T
D. F fluctuating cognitive impairment
E. T

A27.

A. F overtalkativeness
B. F expressive dysphasia
C. F euphoria
D. F tactlessness
E. T

A28.

A. T
B. T

C. T
D. T
E. T

A29.

A. T
B. T
C. T
D. T
E. T

A30.

A. T
B. F   hyposexuality
C. T
D. T
E. T

A31.

A. F   may present with choreiform changes or with dementia
B. F   distractability is a characteristic feature
C. T
D. T
E. T

A32.

A. T
B. T
C. T
D. T
E. T

A33.

A. F   no increased incidence of myocardial infarction
B. T
C. T
D. T
E. T

A34.

A. T
B. T
C. T

D. T
E. T

A35.

A. F a recognised feature of Korsakoff's psychosis
B. T
C. F
D. T
E. T

A36.

A. F onset before the age of 60 years, i.e. Alzheimer's disease is pre-senile dementia
B. F amnesia is usually the presenting feature
C. F EEG changes with increased slow wave activity and decreased alpha rhythm usually seen in early stages of illness
D. F marked loss of performance skills on WAIS
E. T

A37.

A. T
B. F intellectual impairment
C. T
D. F
E. F perforation of the septum pellucidum

A38.

A. T
B. T
C. T
D. T
E. F fluctuating course

A39.

A. F an aspect of the Klüver–Bucy syndrome
B. F dysgraphia
C. F dysfunction of dominant parietal lobe
D. F
E. T

A40.

A. F a feature of dominant parietal-lobe dysfunction
B. F

C. T
D. T
E. T

A41.

A. T
B. T
C. F memory deficits occurring later
D. F personality deterioration occurring early
E. F more common in women

A42.

A. F anterograde amnesia is a good prognostic indicator
B. F neuroses are the commonest psychiatric sequelae
C. T
D. F epilepsy occurs in 5% of closed head injuries
E. F cognitive impairment occurs in 3% of severe injuries

A43.

A. T
B. T
C. T
D. T
E. T

A44.

A. T
B. F insomnia
C. F autonomic overactivity
D. F hypokalaemia
E. F nausea and retching

A45.

A. T
B. F
C. T
D. F
E. F retrograde amnesia

A46.

A. F parietal-lobe syndrome
B. T
C. F parietal-lobe syndrome

D. T
E. F parietal-lobe syndrome

A47.

A. T
B. T
C. F hyperorality
D. F placidity
E. F hypersexuality

A48.

A. T
B. F parietal-lobe syndrome
C. F parietal-lobe syndrome
D. F temporal-lobe syndrome
E. F temporal-lobe syndrome

A49.

A. T
B. T
C. T
D. T
E. T

A50.

A. T
B. F
C. T
D. F
E. T

Paper 4: Questions

Q1. Recognised features of acute organic brain syndrome include

A. inappropriate affect
B. perceptual distortions
C. fluctuating attention
D. delusions
E. non-fluctuating level of consciousness

Q2. Recognised neurological and psychiatric disorders that may develop in hypothyroid patients include

A. schizophrenia
B. depressive disorder
C. subacute organic mental disorder
D. epilepsy
E. acute organic mental disorder

Q3. Recognised features of tabes dorsalis include

A. positive Romberg's sign
B. increased sensitivity to painful stimuli
C. decreased ankle jerks
D. attacks of dull pain
E. paraesthesia

Q4. Causes of Wernicke's encephalopathy include

A. pregnancy
B. carbon monoxide poisoning
C. subarachnoid haemorrhage
D. syphilis
E. post-traumatic

Q5. Recognised features of hepatic encephalopathy include

A. insomnia
B. Babinski response
C. intention tremor
D. labile mood
E. specific EEG changes

Q6. Recognised features of cerebral lupus include

A. depressive psychosis
B. neurotic reactions
C. acute organic disorder
D. chronic organic disorder
E. schizophreniform psychosis

Q7. Recognised features of Alzheimer's disease include

A. epilepsy occasionally
B. visual agnosia
C. logoclonia
D. finger agnosia
E. mirror sign

Q8. Recognised features of Creutzfeld–Jakob disease include

A. flaccidity
B. absence of psychotic features
C. good prognosis
D. dysphagia
E. dysarthria

Q9. Recognised features of communicating hydrocephalus include

A. upper limb motor symptoms
B. cranial nerves may be affected
C. upper limb sensory symptoms occasionally
D. potentially reversible dementia
E. ataxia

Q10. Recognised features of disseminated sclerosis include

A. euphoria
B. dementia
C. lower motor neurone deficits
D. retrobulbar neuritis
E. oculomotor paralysis

Q11. Recognised features of Parkinson's disease include

A. 'clasp knife' rigidity
B. glabellar tap
C. titubation
D. festinant gait
E. intention tremor

Q12. Recognised features of subacute combined cord degeneration include

A. ventral column loss
B. microcytic anaemia
C. lower motor neurone lesions
D. depression
E. dementia

Q13. Recognised features of acute intermittent porphyria include

A. hypotension
B. manic-depressive psychosis
C. delirium
D. epilepsy
E. schizophreniform psychosis

Q14. Recognised features of Pick's disease include

A. dysphasia
B. perseveration
C. early memory deficits
D. early neurological deficits
E. early personality deterioration

Q15. Recognised features of subcortical dementia include

A. occurs in Huntington's chorea
B. apathy
C. occurs in Parkinson's disease
D. depression
E. occurs in progressive supranuclear palsy

Q16. Recognised features of the punch-drunk syndrome include

A. mask-like facies
B. cerebellar lesions
C. persecutory ideation
D. intellectual deterioration
E. personality deterioration

Q17. Recognised features of herpes simplex encephalitis include

A. insidious onset
B. delirium
C. apyrexia
D. focal signs
E. marked hallucinations

Q18. Recognised features of uraemia include

A. functional psychosis commonly
B. seizures occasionally
C. acute delirium in 30%
D. preservation of memory
E. depression

Q19. Recognised features of nicotinic acid deficiency include

A. hallucinations
B. may appear 'hysterical'
C. glossitis
D. confabulation
E. dementia

Q20. Recognised features of transient global amnesia include

A. insidious onset
B. confabulation
C. mild memory impairment
D. alertness
E. impaired personal identity

Q21. Characteristic features of anorexia nervosa include

A. normal BMR
B. hypothermia
C. lanugo hair
D. hypertension
E. phobia of normal body weight

Q22. Common associations with anorexia nervosa include

A. abnormal gastric motility
B. lassitude
C. primary amenorrhoea
D. early morning waking
E. bulimia

Q23. Recognised features of bulimia nervosa include

A. morbid fear of being overweight
B. severe dieting
C. purgative abuse
D. self-induced vomiting
E. binge eating

Q24. Recognised features of bulimia nervosa include

A. euphoria
B. irritability
C. clear signs of starvation
D. anxiety
E. suicidal ideation

Q25. Recognised features of anorexia nervosa include

A. constipation
B. carotenaemia
C. overhydration
D. lethargy
E. lanugo hair on the head

Q26. The following statements are true

A. koro is an acute anxiety state
B. latah is an hysterical reaction to stress
C. windigo is a depressive psychosis
D. susto is an hysterical dissociation or depressive state
E. amok is an acute anxiety state

Q27. The following are true of culture-bound disorders

A. latah features penile retraction into the abdomen
B. piblokto is a dissociative state in Eskimo women
C. windigo involves mutation into a cannibalistic monster
D. koro features automatic obedience, echolalia and echopraxia
E. susto involves loss of the soul

Q28. Recognised features of piblokto

A. seen in Eskimo men
B. a depressive state
C. amnesia only occasionally
D. jumping into water
E. running into the snow

Q29. Recognised features of amok include

A. seen in North American Indian tribes
B. an acute anxiety state
C. homicidal behaviour occasionally
D. more common in men
E. suicidal behaviour may occur

Q30. Recognised features of koro include

A. occurs in women
B. only occurs in Malaysians
C. usually good insight
D. unresolved oedipal conflicts
E. a dissociative state

Q31. Puerperal psychosis has the following features

A. may present within 48 hours of parturition
B. in 40% of cases presents within 7 days of parturition
C. the clinical picture is rarely mixed
D. dominant schizophrenic symptoms indicate a good prognosis
E. is less likely with a family history of affective illness

Q32. Recognised features of 'baby blues' include

A. forgetfulness
B. different illness from the 'maternity blues'
C. affects less than 50% of women within 10 days of parturition
D. despondency
E. can reach the severity of postnatal depression

Q33. Symptoms of combat neurosis include

A. anger
B. grandiose ideas
C. good interpersonal relationships
D. lack of guilt
E. flashbacks

Q34. The fetal alcohol syndrome

A. occurs with as few as four drinks a day
B. causes hydronephrosis
C. causes severe mental retardation
D. causes cleft lip and palate
E. is associated with liver abnormalities

Q35. Encopresis in childhood

A. by definition occurs after age 5
B. has equal sex distribution
C. is more prevalent than enuresis after age 16
D. is always due to constipation
E. may occur in conduct disorder

Q36. Eye to eye contact

A. is usually increased in depression
B. is never a sign of aggression
C. is an essential part of psychotherapy
D. is not influenced by cultural factors
E. is assessed in the mental state examination

Q37. Hollingshead and Redlich

A. published 'Social Class and Mental Illness'
B. based their studies in New York
C. showed that upper class patients tended to use hospitals
D. showed that lower class patients tended to use outpatient clinics
E. are psycho-analysts

Q38. In psychogenic polydipsia

A. polydipsia begins before polyuria
B. vasopressin may relieve thirst
C. urine flow decreases after hypertonic saline infusion
D. urine concentration is greater after vasopressin than after fluid deprivation
E. plasma osmolality is lower than normal

Q39. Recognised features of shell-shock include

A. depersonalisation
B. guilty ideation of delusional intensity
C. derealisation
D. reliving the battle
E. calmness

Q40. The revolving-door syndrome

A. may be due to cerebellar-vestibular dynsfunction
B. is part of the revolving-room syndrome
C. refers to the cyclical re-admission of institutionalised patients
D. generates impressive 'statistics' for 'patient care'
E. rotates patients between system components with adequate care

Q41. With regard to psychiatric illness in general practice

A. hysteria is very common
B. anxiety is relatively uncommon
C. psychotic illness is not usually referred
D. 50% of neurotic illness is usually referred
E. personality disorder is more common than depression

Q42. Recognised features of the typical bereavement reaction include

A. inhibited grief
B. acceptance
C. delayed grief
D. mourning phase
E. chronic grief

Q43. Recognised features of the narcolepsy syndrome include

A. hypnogogic hallucinations
B. hypertonia
C. sleep paralysis
D. catalepsy
E. muscle weakness

Q44. Associations of the depersonalisation syndrome include

A. occurs in emotionally mature
B. specific EEG abnormalities
C. insidious onset
D. occurs usually in middle age
E. occurs in the more intelligent

Q45. Recognised features of atypical grief include

A. feelings of self-blame
B. pseudohallucinations of the deceased
C. searching behaviour
D. illusions
E. misidentifications

Q46. Recognised features of narcolepsy include

A. association with epilepsy
B. equal sex incidence
C. EEG recording similar to normal sleep
D. cataplexy often precipitated by laughter
E. first described by Gélineau in 1912

Q47. Recognised features of shinkeishitsu include

A. obsessional neurosis
B. fear of 'evil eye'
C. mainly affects women
D. occurs in middle age
E. occurs in Japanese

Q48. Recognised features of the episodic dyscontrol syndrome include

A. astereognosis
B. non-specific EEG abnormalities
C. memory impairment
D. an aura following the violent episode
E. lack of remorse for actions

Q49. Recognised features of twilight states include

A. real restriction of consciousness
B. hallucinations
C. abnormal affective states
D. perseveration
E. apparent restriction of consciousness

Q50. Echolalia occurs in

A. catatonia
B. parkinsonism
C. obsessive-compulsive disorders
D. latah
E. mental handicap

Paper 4: Answers

A1.

A. T
B. T
C. T
D. T
E. F fluctuating level of consciousness

A2.

A. T
B. T
C. T
D. T
E. T

A3.

A. T
B. F
C. T
D. F lightning pains
E. T

A4.

A. T
B. T
C. T
D. T
E. T

A5.

A. F hypersomnia
B. F
C. F
D. T
E. F non-specific EEG changes are often an early sign

A6.

A. T
B. T
C. T
D. T
E. T

A7.

A. F epilepsy occurs in 50% of cases
B. T
C. T
D. T
E. T

A8.

A. F spasticity with extensor plantar reflexes
B. F psychotic features are part of the clinical picture
C. F poor prognosis with death occurring within two years
D. T
E. T

A9.

A. F no upper limb motor symptoms
B. F cranial nerves unaffected
C. F no upper limb sensory symptoms
D. T
E. T

A10.

A. T
B. T
C. F upper motor neurone deficits
D. T
E. T

A11.

A. F 'cogwheel' rigidity
B. T
C. T
D. T
E. F 'pill-rolling' tremor (a resting tremor)

A12.

A. F dorsal (posterior) column loss
B. F pernicious anaemia
C. F upper motor neurone lesions
D. T
E. T

A13.

A. F hypertension
B. F schizophreniform psychosis
C. T
D. T
E. T

A14.

A. T
B. T
C. F memory deficits occur later
D. F neurological deficits occur later
E. T

A15.

A. T
B. T
C. T
D. T
E. T

A16.

A. T
B. T
C. T
D. T
E. T

A17.

A. F rapid onset
B. T
C. F pyrexia
D. T
E. T

A18.

A. F functional psychosis occasionally
B. F seizures in 30%
C. T
D. F memory impairment
E. T

A19.

A. T
B. T
C. T
D. T
E. T

A20.

A. F abrupt episode
B. F
C. F global loss of recent memory lasting several hours
D. T
E. F

A21.

A. F
B. T
C. T
D. F hypotension
E. T

A22.

A. F
B. F
C. F amenorrhoea is a primary symptom in a few cases; however, in the majority of cases it is a clinical feature secondary to starvation
D. T
E. T

A23.

A. T
B. T
C. T
D. T
E. T

A24.

A. F
B. T
C. F   body weight usually within normal limits
D. T
E. T

A25.

A. T
B. T
C. F   dehydration
D. F
E. F   lanugo hair on the trunk

A26.

A. T
B. T
C. T
D. F   susto is an acute anxiety state
E. F   amok is an hysterical dissociative state or a depressive state

A27.

A. F   latah features automatic obedience, echolalia and echopraxia
B. T
C. T
D. F   koro features penile retraction into the abdomen
E. T

A28.

A. F   seen in Eskimo women
B. F   an hysterical dissociative state
C. F
D. T
E. T

A29.

A. F   seen in south-east Asia
B. F
C. F   homicidal behaviour frequently
D. T
E. T

A30.

A. T
B. F seen in southern China and Malaya
C. F
D. T
E. F an acute anxiety state

A31.

A. T
B. T
C. F
D. F dominant schizophrenic symptoms indicate a poor prognosis
E. F

A32.

A. T
B. F
C. F affects 50% of women commencing on the 3rd day (postpartum) and lasting for 1 to 2 days
D. T
E. F

A33.

A. T
B. F depressive ideas
C. F poor interpersonal relationships
D. F guilt
E. T

A34.

A. T
B. T
C. F causes mild mental retardation
D. T
E. F

A35.

A. F by definition occurs after age 4
B. F
C. F
D. F
E. T

A36.

A. **F** is usually decreased in depression
B. **F**
C. **F**
D. **F**
E. **T**

A37.

A. **T**
B. **F**
C. **F** showed that upper class patients tended to use outpatient clinics
D. **F** showed that lower class patients tended to use hospitals
E. **F**

A38.

A. **T**
B. **F**
C. **T**
D. **F** urine concentration is greater after fluid deprivation than after vasopressin
E. **T**

A39.

A. **T**
B. **F** guilty ideation not of delusional intensity
C. **T**
D. **T**
E. **F**

A40.

A. **F**
B. **F**
C. **T**
D. **T**
E. **F** rotates patients between system components with inadequate care

A41.

A. **F**
B. **F**
C. **F**
D. **F**
E. **F**

A42.

A. **F** atypical bereavement reaction
B. **T**
C. **F** atypical bereavement reaction
D. **T**
E. **F** atypical bereavement reaction

A43.

A. **T**
B. **F** hypotonia
C. **T**
D. **F** cataplexy
E. **T**

A44.

A. **F**
B. **F**
C. **F** sudden onset
D. **F** occurs usually in adolescence or early adult life
E. **T**

A45.

A. **T**
B. **F** typical grief
C. **F** typical grief
D. **F** typical grief
E. **F** typical grief

A46.

A. **F**
B. **F**
C. **T**
D. **T**
E. **F** first described by Caffé in 1862

A47.

A. **T**
B. **F**
C. **F** mainly affects men
D. **F** occurs in early adult life
E. **T**

A48.

A. T
B. T
C. T
D. F   an aura preceding the violent episode
E. F   remorse for actions

A49.

A. T
B. T
C. T
D. T
E. T

A50.

A. T
B. F
C. F
D. T
E. T